Storefronts and Facades

Book 2

Storefronts and Facades

Book 2

Edited by Martin M. Pegler, SVM

Retail Reporting Corporation New York

Retail Reporting Corporation, 101 Fifth Avenue,
New York, NY 10003

Distributors to the trade in the United States and Canada:
Robert Silver Associates
307 East 37th Street
New York, NY 10016

Distributed outside of the United States and Canada:
Hearst Books International
105 Madison Avenue
New York, NY 10016

Library of Congress Cataloging in Publication Data:
Main Entry under the title: Store Fronts and Facades, Book 2

Printed in Hong Kong
ISBN 0-934590-26-5

Designed by Michael Shroyer

Table of Contents

Introduction

Form and Function are only two of the design elements that are involved in successful store front design. We are not here to debate which comes first—the FORM or the FUNCTION—since often an existing FORM needs to be rehabbed for a new FUNCTION—and in that renovation there is sometimes a revitalization that surpasses the original meeting of FORM and FUNCTION. In addition to these two necessary elements of design there is the FABRICATION; the methods and materials used in the execution of the design which also affects the finished look. Brick, for an example, has been around for centuries and centuries—and though there are traditional methods of bonding,—there are always new ways of combining this material with other materials and textures—or color changes—or shapes and sizes—to create a whole new FINISH for commercial facades.

FENESTRATION is also a determining factor; it is determined by the requirements of the prospective user of the space—and it can determine the ultimate appearance and success of the store front design. Does the client or retailer desire the need for exposure—and light,—or does he require a unique, exclusiveness that demands that the designer "close in" the shop? The degree of FENESTRATION—of the expanse or dearth of glazed areas—will make the statement as to whom is welcome and how welcome they will feel. In the case of Malls, the FENESTRATION may give way to the FREEDOM of Entry and Egress. Is the facade a wide-open, welcoming expression of the FUNCTION of the store or shop—and how is it incorporated into the FORM of the design and into the design format that is often dictated—and enforced by the Mall or Center's management? Thus, continuing with our alliterative journey through the design process—we pass by FORM, FUNCTION, FABRICATION & FINISHES, FENESTRATION & FREEDOM OF ENTRY TO—FASHION, FANCIES & FADS—and also FAMIL-IAR FAVORITES. Sometimes a vogue or fad over-whelms us and we find ourselves expressing our new designs in tried & true vernaculars; we find refuge—and easy communication with the person out in the street—or in the mall—by resorting to cliche decorative elements and designs which, hopefully, are expressed in new and stimulating ways. The old half-timber houses of 15th and 16th century Europe is adapted to the sale of pipes and tobacco. An 18th century, neo-classic entablature seems so right to front a fine men's shop—or a traditional women's shop. A clever adaptation of the kitch, cute Swiss chalet makes an immediate statement for pavement bound skiers who dream of snowy slopes. These familiar favorites can be new and exciting "friends"—well met—when the de-signers combine them with all the other, aforemen-tioned elements into contemporary expressions of today's merchandise and services.

FASHIONS can come and go—and when they return, they are usually as interpretations of what was into what is needed, and they retail the good memories of what was. In our recent "revivals", we find that there is more and more of a return to the ART DECO and the NEO-CLASSIC designs for that inspiration, because they represent something to the shopper out there of what was that they desparately want to recapture—the essence and spirit of the "good times" —something they want to have in their lives.

For our presentation in this volume of outstanding Store Fronts and Facades, we have divided these "Opening Statements" by FORM, FABRICATION & FINISH, FASHION, FAD or FANCY. We feel that the designer or concerned retailer can see how those design elements were used or interpreted, and they can, if they desire, find their own "interpretations" of these concepts to suit their FUNCTION at hand. In some cases we will present facade designs under "Wood"—just to show the many different approaches to the use of wood as a means of FABRICATION, but we will also include wood FINISHED facades in our chapter "Vitruvius, Vignola and VERY Neo-Classic"—to show how Classic elements; entablatures, moldings, and columns,—are expressed in wood as well as in marble—in glass—in metal. We recommend you peruse this volume from A to Z—From ART DECO to ZIG ZAG—to get the feeling of the many, many faces of fronts and facades.

Any editor who calls his volume "The Best of—" is more than dabbling with hubris—he/she is wallowing in egotism. "The Best" means having seen and sampled everything from everywhere, and then,—with the concurrence of all "the best" critics and tastemakers—selecting the "ultimate". We admit to not having been everywhere and having seen everything; we are presenting what we feel is current—is new—is success-ful in interpreting how today's retailer is satisfying his particular target market or customer. These are fronts and facades that more than come out to meet you on Main Streets, side streets, walking streets, Malls, Centers and Strips by the side of the road. They also leave an impression, and they are thus easy to find again—if not in the same mall or on the same street,—then in another town—on another street or in another mall. These fronts and facades make an impression—a lasting one,—and we have attempted to explain what makes them succeed for the retailer—and the people he/she seeks to reach.

Enjoy your "walk" through many streets, centers and cities,—in the U.S. and abroad—and may you come back many, many times to find "inspiration" and "ideas"—for your own interpretations.

Martin M. Pegler, S.V.M.
Editor

Contemporary

The front of a retail store serves several functions. It acts as a symbol of the store—its merchandise and philosophy, and it is an attraction to draw shoppers to the store. It must give the shopper an unmistakable impression of the store's price range, product, service, selection, degree of sales assistance, level of quality, and type of shopper the store is attempting to attract. The storefront performs this task through properly selected materials, signs, views to the interior, product display, and entrance control. The designer and the retailer have complete control over what passers-by see within the store. The storefront acts both as a filter to screen out store elements the designer does not wish the shopper to see, such as service areas, and as a lens to focus attention on the products for sale. Finally, the storefront is a transition area between mall to the store itself. This transition space must meet the expectations of the shopper. If a customer expects exclusivity, the transition must be designed to control the flow of people into the store. If the shopper expects the store to attract the general public, the transition into the store must be easy and open.

William R. Green
Green Hiltscher Shapiro, Ltd., Chicago, IL
Exerpted from ''The Retail Store'' by William R. Green
Copyright 1987 - Van Nostrand Reinhold Co.

Contemporary = ''of the same time'' or ''existing''. It is what we think of when someone says ''Today''—''Up-to-date''. Contemporary is ''Modern'' and ''modern'' is ''Characteristic of present or recent times,—not antiquated or obsolete''. It is more than straight lines and sharp angles; it is clean, classy and current. Contemporary is the current state of our art affairs—the ''state of the art'' of design. It is new materials mixed with older materials in a melange of neat, orderly and often sleek designs; not heavy on trim or ornament—not embellished or enriched—but straightforward and simple. The accent is on Simplicity. In this chapter we treat CONTEMPORARY as something separate and apart from HIGH TECH and STRUCTURAL—which are also part of today's design vernacular—and are represented in a chapter of their own. The POST MODERN movement is another form of the ''contemporary'', and it, too, is represented later on in this volume. When we address the CONTEMPORARY store fronts and facades, we are considering the designs that, without all that Jazz and Pizzazz, are making Opening Statements that are relevant to today's retailers—and their customers.

Here, the emphasis is on creating a separation between what is outside and what is inside—and yet facilitate the movement in and out. These designs more than suggest what is inside,—they make it visible to the passerby. What they add up to is an unfussy, clean and direct approach to store design with lots of glass—metallic accents and sometimes facades that are only fascias that carry the store's name and/or logo—and little else. Spartan—but not sterile, crisp—but not cold; it is commerce with class.

Foleys, South Park Drive, Corpus Christi, TX   Architect: Lloyd Jones Assoc., Houston, TX

Department stores as well as specialty stores need to make an image statement—up front. On this page: two leading chains of department stores show their current, contemporary, "now-look"—architecturally. The architects have combined clean straight lines with gentle arcs and curves that seem to wrap around and invite the shopper to enter. Shopping malls are often the setting for night-time shopping experiences, and lighting counts. The lighting therefore becomes a major element in the architectural design and affects how the forms and shapes are integrated into the facade design. Right: two mall-enclosed specialty stores,—also in balanced arrangements of straight lines and welcoming curves. These stores exist in a no-daylight situation and thus rely on the external and internal lighting to enhance the facing materials—make the signage visible—and create the proper impression.

Rich's, Riverchase Galleria, Hoover, AL
Architect: Hambrecht Terrell International, NY

Leeds & Sons, Desert Fashion Plaza, Palm Springs, CA
Architect: Harwood K. Smith

Jacques Schiesser, Stamford Town Center, Stamford, CT
Architect: Stephen Sanders & Assoc., Manhasset, NY

A play of lines;—verticals and horizontals in a geometric latticework that holds panes of glass in sharply defined rectangular spaces. The entrance is clearly outlined and emphasized; there is no confusion as to where one enters. Jane Aubert's facade is all glass with a massive entrance design that telescopes towards the actual swinging doors of the shop—creating a foyer in the transition. Cherry Lane's design could almost be a Mondrian painting realized in black metal and glass with an asymmetrical balance in the display windows. Adler's jewelry store is formal, symmetrical,— perfectly balanced in keeping with the fine jewelry contained in the museum cases in the two windows. Here, the materials used mix the subtle gleam of the stainless steel tubes that protect the glass windows and outline the base of those windows with the deep gray, baked enamel finish. A thinner tube with a chromed finish frames the windows and the door.

Cherry Lane, Beverly Center, Los Angeles, CA

Adler, Geneva, Switzerland

A to Z, Durbrook Mall, Humble, TX
Architect: Walker Group/CNI, NY

Getting a fresh slant on the contemporary facade. Diagonal lines replace the more formal verticals for a dynamic feeling—a sense of excitement—of action. Gene Raymond (left) is a trendy, young men's, high fashion shop on the evolving Melrose Ave. in Los Angeles. The facade of the rehabbed building becomes immediately recognizable as the strong, slanting black metal tubes create a triangular window space in an otherwise no-color, textured stucco front. A to Z's facade uses the diagonals to "close-in" the entrance,—to make a more intimate statement while not losing any of its wide-open exposure. It is also almost a replay of the diagonals in the letters A and Z. The Midland Bank keeps its financial "dignity"—but the formality of the verticals and the horizontals present a foil for the dominant "V" shaped logo that appears in the window and is viewable in the interior. Note the effective night lighting.

Midland Bank, Bristol, Great Britain
Architect: Fitch & Co., London, Great Britain

Raspini's, Boynton Beach Mall, Boynton Beach, FL

Set-backs,—step-backs,—movement in line. Raspini's design of "floating" horizontal, wood shelves is capped with a horizontal canopy that carries the name in bright metal. The up front design is balanced by strong verticals—near the clearly defined open entrance. The end result is an interesting interplay of planes—of divided spaces. Ann Taylor's canopy makes a strong "V" shaped thrust into the line of traffic of the high-traffic mall, and the shopper can see the name from either direction. The "V" is repeated even more emphatically in the white ceramic tile floor that goes out to meet the darker flooring of the mall. The Club House manages to be seen even in the relatively dark corner because the corrugated overhang takes advantage of the daylight to create an exciting, directional zig-zag into the store. The canopy over Robinson's is supported by slender columns and becomes just one more horizontal plane in the fascinating cluster of cubes that have been organized into a monumental facade.

Ann Taylor, Horton Plaza, San Diego, CA
Architect: Charles E. Broudy & Assoc., Philadelphia, PA

The Club House, Town Center, Boca Raton, FL

Robinson's, Fashion Valley, San Diego, CA

Ballys of Switzerland, South Coast Plaza, Costa Mesa, CA   Architect: Hambrecht Terrell International, NY

Horizontal lines stretch while vertical lines add dignity and height. The Bally store front is a handsome mixture of brass moldings and beige marble veneer with the Bally logo, also in brass, applied to the marble wall. The windows are simply framed but the pattern of assorted rectangles,—like the Mondrian designs previously mentioned, make the entrance noteworthy. Black marble vertical fins meet and pass under the long black mirror fascia that stretches across the multi-angled facade of Ann Taylor. Each fin creates a separate "window"—a separate bay for viewing. The dominant entrance design serves as the fulcrum and balances the bays on the left with their mirror image on the right. In-Wear Matinique almost assumes the weightiness of an Egyptian mastaba. The smooth, white stucco facade —germane to the mall—is enlivened with the incised lines that are accented with stainless steel strips. The entrance gets special architectural attention and it seems to step forward from the flanking windows. Illuminated signage is embedded in the band over the entrance.

Ann Taylor, Owings Mill, Baltimore County, MD   Architect: Charles E. Broudy & Assoc., Philadelphia, PA

In Wear-Matinique, Town Center, Boca Raton, FL

High Tech &
Skeletal Structures

"Frequently, the strength of the 'inviting pull' of a unique storefront design or the excitement of the merchandise presentation within can mean the difference in whether a customer will look *at a store, let alone* enter *it in the 5-7 seconds they take to pass it.*

"The store's front is a business card; an immediate image statement; a three-dimensional advertisement that must instantly describe the product at a glance. This is done through architectural design, display and/or merchandise presentation.

"With recent trends toward total vision into the store and the elimination of enclosed display statements, the entire store becomes the storefront. This allows the merchandise to be more responsible for setting the stage and communicating the store's image, letting the customer know this is 'my' store. It also gives the store the 'chameleon element'; the ability to change its look overnight. This versatility establishes an effective vehicle for reacting to consumer trends and business developments without sacrificing individuality."

Kenneth E. Nisch, President
Jon Greenberg and Associates, Inc.

I t all seems to have begun back in 1851, in England, when Joseph Paxton created the Crystal Palace to commemorate and house examples of the fruits of the Industrial Revolution. Using everyday, utilitarian, prefabricated parts—and based on the ridge and furrow construction that was popular in greenhouse construction, Paxton designed a glittering, glass structure that contained 800,000 sq. ft. of exhibition space. The Palace was a fantasy of iron bars, beams, struts and trusses and four foot sheets of glass—the largest size available at that time. Using the mundane he created the magnificent,—he turned the usual into the unique and "fathered" what we today refer to as High Tech. It is the celebration of Industrial elements turned into works of art by the creative artist.

Today, everywhere in the world, there are new, high tech Crystal Palaces appearing as shopping centers and malls—as department store facades. Since we are once again carrying the sun's light onto the selling floor, the atrium has almost become a "standard" in the mega-stores being built. Once again, the soaring expanse of glass are held in place within a fine grid of metal—and the web of glass and steel that spans the store's interior brings back memories of Paxton's Palace of over 100 years ago—the breath-taking 19th cent. railroad terminals of Europe—and our own, now sadly lost, Penn Station, in N.Y.

In this chapter we have combined structural systems and construction modules with the glass encased fantasies to show another "face" of retailing.

Greenway, Shop Rite Plaza, Yonkers, NY
Design: Planned Expansion Group, White Plains, NY

Square One Shopping Center,
Mississauga, Ont. Canada
Developer: Murray Marshall & Creswell

Stevens Creek Valley Fair, San Jose, CA
Developer: Kober Group

Mayfair Mall, Milwaukee, WI

The construction becomes the design; beams, girders and interlacing, intertwining rods create webs, cats-cradles, and an infinite number of shapes, shadows and pattern-plays. It is the Crystal Palace of 1851 updated— in new materials—and it flies to new heights—capturing and enveloping glazed panels of sizes then undreamed of. Whether used only as a contemporized version of the multipaned fan windows of the 18th century—or as a total oversized "green-house" that spreads out to nurture acres of retail establishments,—the skeletal structures are the design statement. The "fan window" motif is reinterpreted on the left in the entrances to two shopping malls. At the Square One Shopping Center the architect provided a soaring porte-cochere in the shape of an arch with a fan window enclosure backed up by a second ascending arch—also with radiating panels of glass—that repeat the fan window design. Below: Stevens Creek Valley Fair uses a giant "tinker-toy" technique to enhance a brick and stone building. Mayfair (above) is one of many variations of the "green-house" variety—even to the slanted glazed roofs that take advantage of the daylight—all day long.

The Complete Athlete, Westside Pavilion, Los Angeles, CA   Design: Wayne Berg, NY

Cubes and boxes—arches—columns—diagonal struts; it's all construction—and these shops are all different. The Complete Athlete is almost formal in its symmetry and with the tubular columns that support the wire-framed, mesh arch. The arch motif is repeated inside over the main open space. The boxed-in windows are set back in a corrugated design. Champs is full of diagonals—filled with action and movement and the bright red enamel finish adds to the sense of excitement. United Status Apparel has its cube-on-cube entrance design enhanced with red neon outlines. The same red delineates the all important first letters in the sign. The balance of the facade is also boxed off with wide black metal bands. The minute jewelry shop, Aspasis, makes a big presence with the open grid facade and the diagonal line that slashes across the repetitious design. The grid of the front is a replay of the tile patterned floor of the mall.

Champs, Owings Mills,
Baltimore County, MD

Aspasia, Trumbull Shopping Park, Trumbull, CT
Design: Steven Bezas Design, Huntington, NY

United Status Apparel, Town & Country, Kendall, FL

The Gallery, Baltimore Harbour, MD
Developer: The Rouse Co.

26

Moorestown Mall, Moorestown, NJ
Developer: Goodman, Segar Hogan, Inc.

The Galleria is a new addition to Baltimore's
Harborside spread of retail shops but this glass
enclosure goes up to become part of the new skyline.
There is an exciting play of angles and shapes—cuts
and facets—glass contained in a metal framework—all
unified and contained in a "tinkertoy" outer skeleton.
It is what's outside that counts! The corner entrance
makes a sparkling faceted statement—like a sun
rise—or Miss Liberty's crown. The interior is bathed
with daylong day-light. The Moorestown Mall is
fronted with a cut-crystal facade; glazed panels and
angled roofs. The forward, three storey tower angles
into the street for a strong presence. At night, the tower
glows with interior illumination and becomes a beacon
for evening shoppers.

Arjan, Beverly Center, Los Angeles, CA

Schatz, Trumbull Shopping Park, Trumbull, CT
Architect: Jon Greenberg and Assoc., Berkley, MI

Metal cubes and ladders as well as trellises of square metal are used in these store facades. Schatz's open front is contained within a proscenium of rectangular openings of gray blue enameled tubing. Inside the store, the same proscenium motif is used on the floor for visual merchandising and thus the front and interior are integrated into a single, complete design. At Arjan, a structural metal tube trellis frames the entrance. Once inside, the same structural system boxes off the walls and serves as the method for holding and showing merchandise. Galtier Plaza is a glittering glass tower by night and the glazed enclosure glows with interior illumination—and overflows with the evening excitement from within. In this super modern structure one still discerns the classic motifs that are so popular in so many of todays design solutions.

Galtier Plaza, St. Paul, MN

Neo-Classics

Successful stores are the result of a combination of many elements including, in order of importance: the retailing expertise of the merchant/owner; the interior planning and, merchandising; the interior lighting design; and, last, the exterior building design. Yet it is only the design of the building facade which communicates the owner's public image *to the community at large. It should, therefore, be a faithful expression of the way the owner wants to be perceived by customers. The facade design must establish a unique identity for the retailer. If the designer meets this objective and the merchant is successful, the customer will associate the combination of merchandising and exterior design as a single identity labeled by the public as a "great store".*

Leo Martinez, Principal
Cole Martinez Curtis and Associates
Marina Del Rey, CA

Designs can be in "fashion", but being "fashionable" doesn't guarantee long lasting acceptance. Fads and Fancies are even more ephemeral—more fleeting—than Fashion. Some designs go on forever and ever—delivering the right message; they tell it like it is meant to be and they don't wilt or lose their dewy freshness. The Classic elements of Architecture of Vitruvius and Vignola go on and on, and though they may be artfully altered or adapted by succeeding generations of architects and designers,— the original message still comes through. The familiar Doric, Ionic and Corinthian columns with their capitols—simple or heavily embellished—still say "class", "elegance", "refinement"—and "traditional". The architectural entablatures and moldings reiterate a lasting and on-going quality—a "from now till forever" sense of dependability that seems so suited to certain types of retail establishments. The Classic elements become the Neo-Classic and the neo, Neo-Classic as time goes on but "age cannot wither her nor custom stale her infinite variety"—or the intent of the design elements.

In the following examples we will see the Column used to add a strong vertical line to an otherwise horizontal scheme; suggesting elegance and strength— as well as the reassurance of permanence. It says— "Our merchandise is timeless"—"You are investing in the future". Arches make graceful swoops over doorways and windows—creating colonnades and miniature shopping arcades that are a fresh-eyed adaptation of 17th and 18th century retail architecture. Pedimented doorways, corbel enriched facades and fascias embellished with carved moldings all seem comfortable and secure in contemporary shopping malls or facing the traffic on Main St. After succeeding for over 2000 years, it's hard to believe that the Classic elements can be or will be intimidated by today's retailers—or the shoppers who are looking for lasting value.

Collins & Aikman, The Merchandise Mart, Chicago, IL   Design: Eva Maddox Assoc., Chicago, IL   Photo: Orlando Cabanban

Britches, Owings Mill, Baltimore County, MD

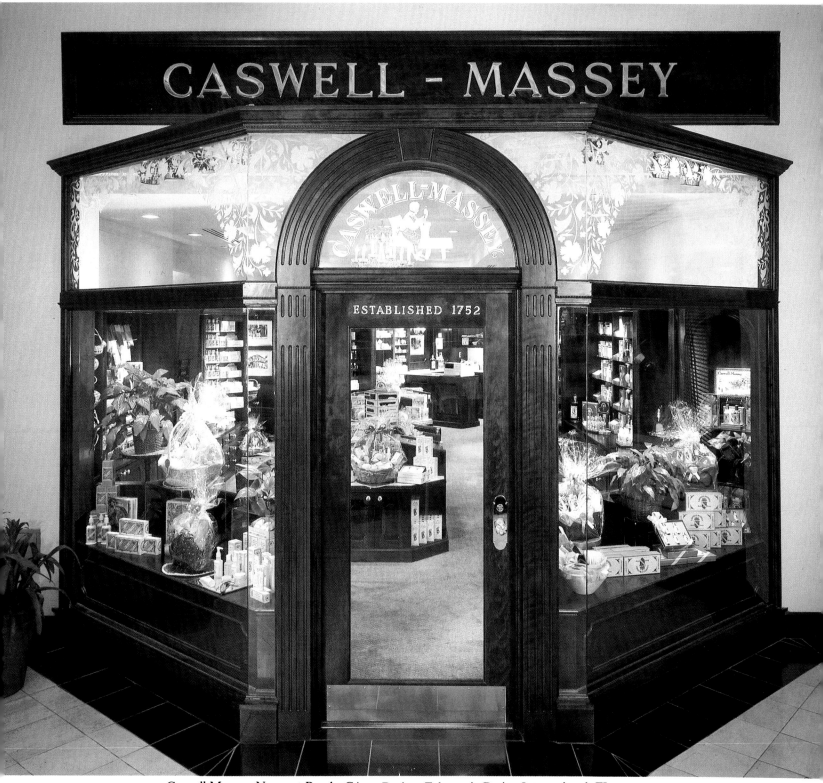

Caswell Massey, Newport Beach, CA   Design: Echeverria Design International, FL

Neo Classic Revisited—and updated. The arched openings and the fan windows just reviewed in High Tech constructions takes on a sleek elegance when it is executed in rich, polished wood. The Collins & Aikman showroom speaks the neo-classic lines with a contemporary accent and the designers have reiterated the facade statement as a decorative motif inside the shop—adding depth and drama to the limited space. The Caswell-Massey corner shop makes effective use of the arched shape to make an important entrance in a rather small facade. Wooden moldings and panels are combined with the clear and etched glass to state the company's English heritage,—the tradition and "class" of the shop and the merchandise. Britches makes a strong, sweeping statement in the massive bowed entrance with arced windows on either side. Up front, a very neo-classically inspired, corbel-supported entablature holds the inverted marble veneered half circle that bears the store's primary sign.

Topaz, Roosevelt Field, Garden City, NY
Architect: Martin Dorf Assoc., NY

Right: two examples of the pedimented arch—in two interpretations. The Bombay Shop uses the finely scaled and detailed arch as the entrance into the shop and to introduce its mahogany reproductions of 18th century furniture and accessories. The balance of the facade is glass and marble with a self-illuminated sign on the fascia over the door. Gary's Tux Shop borrows the style and elegance inherent in the neo-classic look to upscale the formal wear within. In the midst of the art deco and pop explosion of colors surrounding this

shop, the overscaled details like the dentil course and the channeling in the piers manage to suggest the desired dignity and yet exist in the playfulness and exaggeration all around. Topaz (above) presents an unobstructed view into the contemporary shop. The neo-classic, rusticated front seems to be composed of raised chamfered stone panels organized into a vertical support for the stone lintel with the very visible store name. The block on block motif continues inside the store.

The Bombay Shop, Owings Mill,
Baltimore County, MD

Gary's Tuxedo Shop, Horton Plaza,
San Diego, CA

Mark Cross, South Coast Plaza, Costa Mesa, CA

The arch marches on! The wood lined interior of Mark Cross is visible through the wood outlined facade. The main entrance is guarded by a pair of cannelated piers and crowned with a fan window. The signage appears on the wood fascia that divides the window glass. Below: Ricarde takes the Palladian motif and turns it into a store front opening. The two slender colonnettes divide the space into three and the arch, complete with keystone, above points up the main walk-through. The period inspired "cabinet" is part of the facade design and serves as the display window. The dark stained columns and the heavily molded doors and archway that lead into Chico's are artfully counterpointed against the cool aqua tinted entrance recess. The balance of the facade is relaxed and contemporized with the natural pine planks that sheath the walls and valances over the windows which have also been highlighted and "lightened-up" with aqua moldings.

Ricarde, Canal Place, New Orleans, LA

Chico's, The Esplanade, Palm Beach, FL

Goldi's, Woodfield Mall, Schaumberg, IL
Design: Kubala-Washatko, Cedarberg, WI
Photo: Mark Heffron, Milwaukee, WI

As classically inspired as almost any major government building in Washington D.C.—or in the Acropolis is Goldi. It starts off with a truly classic colonnade of faux marble columns supporting a molding enriched entablature of a most unclassic shrimp-pink. A second colonnade is set behind—part of the store facade and part of the store interior. The "broken" column allows an open look to the rear of this most unique shop. Neoclassic pediments create merchandising bays on the left wall of the store. The facade "moves" forward —almost to the building line of the mall—but on an angle that gets attention—and draws the shopper in. The "split" marble flooring brings the store interior right out into the mall.

SOME WALLS *JUST* HOLD UP CEILINGS.

WALLSELL

SYSTECH

Our Walls Bring Up Sales.

Ever notice how some stores have walls that just stand there? They're not increasing sales. They're not creating excitement. They're not from Columbus Show Case.

Wall systems from Columbus Show Case, on the other hand, are specifically designed to fit your store's image, your store's merchandise, and your store's exact physical dimensions.

For example, our WallSell System. It can give a whole new shape and look to your store, while still accommodating your existing hardware. Our WallSell perimeter system accommodates a wide array of standard or custom panels. The pre-engineered framework incorporates changing wall conditions and provides for a rapid and clean installa-

tion. Freestanding WallSell gives you new freedom to move walls into the selling area. Plus, Columbus Show Case offers 10-day turnaround on painted vinyl panels and most standard laminated panels.

The totally modular Systech System offers an even more individualized answer to your needs. We work closely with you in custom-designing hardware, panel finish and corresponding floor units. The result creates a completely integrated design...a design that will be yours and yours alone.

To find out more, just drop us a line. Or call our marketing communications department, at 1-800-848-3573. We'll be happy to give you a free design proposal for your specific merchandising needs.

COLUMBUS SHOW CASE, WE SELL WALLS THAT SELL.

COLUMBUS SHOW CASE COMPANY
850 West Fifth Avenue ■ Columbus, Ohio 43212 ■ (614) 299-3161

Post Modern Models

Whether it is the permanent building front or a newly created effect, a facade makes the first impression to your customer. A facade is like the wrapping around a package; it evokes a customer's imagination as to what's inside and influences how they feel about going in.

The entry makes a statement through volume and spacial relationships. Some facades are warm and welcoming (the Elizabeth Arden red door). Others have a powerful scale and create drama (Tiffany's Gilberti style doors).

A facade can also be used as a strong communication device to present a product or story. By staging a presentation of merchandise or a fashion theme, the facade can give a statement that allows shoppers to mentally move beyond the front of the store.

In approaching the design of a retail facade, we first establish the approach, its relationship to its environment, adjoining structures, the selected site and the message our client wants to convey.

The creative develops through an exploration of ideas which address the desired image of our client, the point of entry, visual display opportunities and the architectural vocabulary. Through this expression, a unique personality and distinct sense of place emerge to identify our client to their audience.

Eva L. Maddox, President
Eva Maddox Assoc., Inc.
Chicago, IL

While purists agree and architects take sides, we find many talented designers intrigued with the imaginative possibilities of the Post Modernism Movement—and they forge forward with new contemporized store fronts and facades that use arches and columns and color as they haven't been used for some time. After a starvation diet of years of Spartan, unadorned and unembellished architectural creations, we now see a swelling out of curves and color,—of controlled enrichments on otherwise clean, contemporary facades. The noted architect and educator, Paul Rudolf said, "I think buildings should look backwards as well as forwards, just as people do. Ornament can be used to give meaning to buildings by associating them with history, literature, social movements, etc." "Post Modernism seeks to restore a broader range of architectural forms and meanings through the use of ornament, cultural symbols, and historical references,—all of which the Modernists had discarded", says Andrea Oppenheimer Dean in an issue of Smithsonian.

In this chapter we present some modern facades that have gone beyond; looked forward and backwards —used contemporized variations of old motifs and ornaments to make their facades special and memorable.

The Broadway, South Coast Plaza, Costa Mesa, CA
Architect: Architects Pacifica, Newport Beach, CA
Store Design: Cole Martinez Curtis and Assoc., Marina del
Rey, CA

In the ever-expanding South Coast Plaza several
noteworthy California department stores have staked
their reputations with buildings that are monumental in
size and heroic in detail. The almost unadorned mass of
textured concrete blocks that face The Broadway
suddenly give way to a gigantic semi-circular arched
entrance way—fronted with circular planters and easy-
to-climb, terraced steps. The arch motif is repeated over
and over again—funneling back to the actual entrance
and the sweeping fan window that extends over the full
bank of doors below. The collection of diminishing
arches is faced with large mosaic tiles that catch and
reflect the light. A stepped down pattern, on the left,
compensates for the incline in the plot.

Nordstrom's, South Coast Plaza, Costa Mesa, CA
Architect: Steve Harmon, A.I.A.
Store Design: The Callison Partnership, Seattle, WA

Nordstrom's glows against the bright blue California sky,—the two tones of reddish brick accented with the pink stone highlights. A "frame" has been cut out of the cube-like front and a post-modern "triumphal arch" of pink stonework has been set into the opening. The sweeping arch is supported on two multiple columns joined by square neckings. The shopper steps down—under the arch—and the store name which has been carved on the stone panel over the doors. Above the sign—another sweep of arch—this one glazed.

Inside, the entire upper level consists of arch after arch spanning the open atrium—and the round columns with square neckings are also repeated. The store's facade makes an impressive statement—for the store's image—and its fashion image. For the visitor to South Coast Plaza, this store offers an interesting arrangement of blocks and masses—shadows and highlights—that change in their relationships with the moving sun.

Express: Westwood, Los Angeles, CA

Belladonna: The Promenade, Singapore

A brushed stainless steel arch rests on two metal wrapped columns with bright shiny rings that serve as caps and bases. That bit of shimmer and shine designates the entrance to Express. On the left, a giant "oeil de boeuf" (bull's eye) is an on-target opening through which the shopper can shop the excitement within. The window on the right is capped with an arch to match the entrance design. Belladonna has an all glass facade but a free-standing, post-modern inspired arch with squared columns (actually merchandising units) creates the opening impression. The columns are used throughout the shop and the color scheme of the entrance arch is restated too. David Orgell sells fine jewelry and silver and is well known in the up-scale market. This post-modern collaboration of a weighty marble arch, round, uncapped columns and massive square bases,—combined with the updated fan window and metal mullioned doors makes an impactful front face.

David Orgell, South Coast Plaza, Costa Mesa, CA

The Broadway, Horton Plaza, San Diego, CA
Horton Plaza Architect: The Jerde Partnership, LA, CA
Graphic Design & Color: Sussman/Prejza, Santa Monica, CA

The bright colors,—the happy mix and match of
arches, rectangles, keystones, balustrades and details
reinterpreted in new ways are all part of the commercial
excitement of Horton Plaza, and The Broadway store
rising over the many terraced levels. The up-to-the-
minute conceit of a fan-window gets a free-for-all
treatment in color and design and makes a brave
presence that carries the store name over the eclectic
shopfronts around it. The Town Center at Cobb sweeps
forward with a look into the 21st century with a
semilune canopy of glass and metal strips resting on a
pink concrete structure of rectangular openings and
squared arches. The wall behind consists of squares
within squares with squared modules "missing" to
make an interesting stepped profile.

Town Center at Cobb, Cobb County, GA   Developer: Cadillac Fairview   Architect: RTKL Assoc.

J.W. Robinson, South Coast Plaza, Costa Mesa, CA

J.W. Robinson adds its own particular post-modern imprint on the South Coast Plaza. Next door to The Broadway and just a turn or two from Nordstrom's, the three are so compatible in their architectural designs and yet so different in their sum totals. The blockish front is like its neighbor, yet the arch cut out of the square and the rounded columns are reminiscent of Nordstrom's entrance. Where The Broadway's facade is off center and asymmetrically balanced, this front is formal and symmetrical. Godchaux/Maison Blanche combines the old with the new in this facade which is really an arcaded portico—a Renaissance shopping concept updated for a part of the country rich in tradition—and European ways. It is a bit of Rue Royale transported to Louisiana. The portico serves as a weather guard for the shoppers and also cuts down the heat of the sun—and it can get hot down there.

Godchaux/Maison Blanche, Baton Rouge, LA
Architect: Hambrecht Terrell International, NY

The Lakeside Delicatessen, Oakland, CA
Design: Ace Architects, Oakland, CA
Photo: Russell Abraham, San Francisco, CA

Three stimulating store fronts full of swirling lines—neon lights and memories of a classic past. The Lakeside Delicatessen takes its early Roman design heritage and reinterprets the pediment as a neon broken triangle, and the capless columns twirl down to flat bases. The facade bows out and unifies the two entrances with a glazed center area. Figaro spells out "fun" from its black tile front. The cut out arch becomes a barrell vault inside and the two rondels frame neon signs. The spiralling columns are painted silver and set into the black and white tile floor which appears as part of the shop front. The splash of red neon glow across the front makes a vibrant sign. Dimitrios is set inside a mall where the other two face out onto streets. The very effective front is a combination of shiny black and white sparked with bright red—and checkerboard patterns mixing it up with swirling ribbon patterns. The arched mirror fascia is illuminated from behind and the shop name reads strong and clear. The facade and the store interior are inseparable—indivisible.

Figaro, Oakland, CA
Design: Ace Architects, Oakland, CA
Photo: Rob Super

Dimitrios, Columbus, OH   Design: Lidia Danjell Design, Columbus, OH   Photo: Jeff Rycus

Walter Pyes, Memorial City Mall, Houston, TX   Design: Richard Roeder Assoc., Houston, TX

Galt Toys, Woodfield Mall, Schaumberg, IL   Design: Schafer Assoc., Oakbrook, IL   Photo: Jim Norris

Eclectic Elegance

From the nineteen fifties, sixties and well into the seventies, storefronts and criteria were created by consultants who knew little of presenting a merchant and his goods. Sterile controls with sanitized storefront criteria were hoisted onto chain stores, who expanded with the shopping centres from coast to coast (in some cases the developer actually created the chain store). The storefront and signage were secondary compared to the actual store openings, besides storefronts cost much too much (particularly, corner locations), when compared cost-wise to the interior store fixturing and lighting.

The storefront is back, the sterile shopping centre revolution is over. A new age with the storefront respondent in evocative signage announcing the merchants marketplace position and quality of merchandise has arrived, together with the total concept of merchandise and space.

R. MacLachlan, ISP, ARIDO, IDC, Exec. Vice President
The International Design Group
Toronto, Ont.

ECLECTIC: "noting or pertaining to works of architecture and/or decoration produced during a certain period that derive from a wide range of historic styles, the style in each instance being chosen for its fancied appropriateness to the purpose being served or the cultural background of the client". Or, simply stated: "made up of what is selected from different sources." It is bits and pieces of Yesterday's Fashions and Fancies,—reincarnated and reinterpreted to invest contemporary facades with the spirit of the original's charm or what they represented. It can be the mix and match of different motifs—from different times—blended by the materials selected and how the designer uses them. It is Retro Time; a return to the past,—not necessarily the "long departed" past—but a time that today personifies a certain "look" and makes a particular fashion statement. Among the by-gone styles that reach out to today's shoppers are Art Deco, Art Nouveau, the Streamline of the '40s and the Innocence of the '50s.

In an Eclectic design, the designer doesn't slavishly imitate or reproduce the period or fashion as an entity, but, selects those elements that seem to be the essence of the time and then work that into the new design—using it to impart a particular message and by inference suggest the glamour—the giddiness—the svelte sophistication that was inherent in that period of time. Thus, our selection of selective backward looks—brought forward into today.

Luciano Donna, Dadeland, Miami, FL   Architect: Echeverria Design International, FL

Art Deco is alive and well and willing to be used where fashionable elegance needs to be expressed. Luciano Donna mates marble with glass—plus brass and accents of gold. The design is symmetrical and restrained but a fine opening remark for the glamour that resides within. The brass insets in the black marble floor outlines the faceted windows and becomes an entrance aisle. Wallach & Sons is represented by a simple sweep of brushed copper above and a balanced base to match. The small shop front is divided into three parts by the metal moldings that encase the glazed door. Camille is simple marble and brass, but the grillwork on the door is based on a Parisian art deco original. The doorway makes a "selective" statement; anybody can look in but not everybody can afford to come in. Miss Maud is glass but the circle within a circle dominates and draws the shoppers attention to the black metal lines that become the vertical patterned doors of this shoe shop. The name is discreetly painted, at eye level, on the glass.

Wallach & Sons, The Americana, Manhasset, NY

Camille, Mayfair-in-the Grove, Coconut Grove, FL   Architect: Echeverria Design International, FL

Miss Maud, The Americana, Manhasset, NY

55

Laise Adzer, Horton Plaza, San Diego, CA

At Laise Adzer, a moorish influence makes itself known in the bronze and white ceramic tiled facade—a medley of chevrons and stripes. The inner surfaces of the entry posts seem to converge as they approach the flat lintel over the door. White washed Corinthian columns flank the entrance and frame the window—also painted white. The Moorish-motif is even more pronounced in the Laise Adzer shop on the far right where the shopper passes through a white, horse-shoe arch on the natural faience tiled floor. Within, the North African arches divide the shop into shopping bays. Burdines welcomes shoppers into The Florida Store with illuminated palm trees that start out as semi-Egyptian lotus capped columns. The cloud filled sky that overflows the ceiling, a la Tiepolo, becomes the fascia that carries the illuminated sign. A whip-last line—a nouveau interpretation of Art Nouveau—becomes a unique, off-centered, glass contained arch opening into the Aspasia jewelry store. The balance of the design is wood, mirror and glass in clean right-angled lines.

Burdines, Coral Square, Coral Springs, FL   Architect: Heery & Heery, Atlanta, GA   Store Design: Walker Group/CNI, NY

Laise Adzer, Beverly Center, Los Angeles, CA   Design: Laise Adzer

Aspasia, The Galleria,
White Plains, NY

57

Sara Fredericks Short Hills Mall, NJ   Design: Alan Barnouw Design Katonah, NY

Beyond, Town Center, Boca Raton, FL

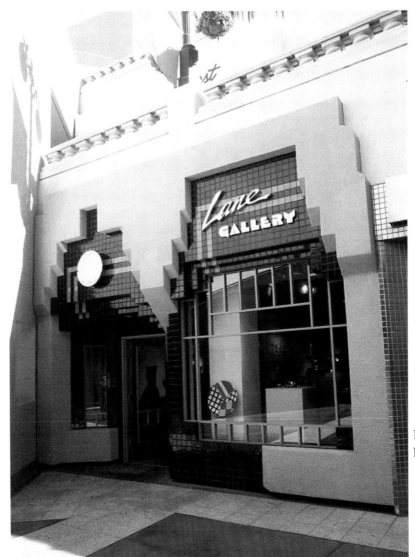

Lane Gallery, Horton
Plaza, San Diego, CA

59

Modern Jewelers, Fairoaks Mall, Fairfax, VA   Developer: The Taubman Co., Bloomfield Hills, MI

The twenties and thirties reappear in Modern Jewelers black mirror and chrome striped facade. It is patterned and designed to flow from one end to the other— and the stripes which are so important to the look move from the exterior into and around the shop—and back out at the other end. The style of lettering used also recalls the "Moderne" of the 30s. Pace has taken its corner location and turned it into a "work of art" with an acknowledged bow to Mondrian and Leger. The metal canopy makes an S-sweep over the doorway which otherwise blends with the wrap-around window design. Touches of patinad copper add to the architectural conceit. Montana—a Mecca on Rodeo Drive—makes a stylish Retro statement with the glass block front borrowed from the 40s. The blocks are contained in a sophisticated architectural framework that makes the right "up" impression for the merchant —the merchandise—and the shopper.

Pace Collection, Madison Ave., NY

Montana, Rodeo Drive, Los Angeles, CA

Cacharel, The Bourse, Philadelphia, PA

Henry Birks & Son, Toronto, Ont., Canada   Architect: International Design Group, Toronto

Hot Spots!

Trappers Alley, Detroit, Michigan

Downtown Detroit's Historic Festival Marketplace located in Greektown. Opened in 1985, **Trappers Alley** has received numerous design and construction awards, and enjoys its position as a shopping and dining experience to the 5th strongest convention city in the country.

Rainbow Centre ULC Award-winning multi-level successful retail and dining complex adjacent to magnificent Niagara Falls, New York.

The Centre, Park Forest A Chicago, Illinois, suburban mall featuring Marshall Fields, Sears, and a variety of specialty shops in the unique, lush surroundings of a European marketplace.

Charleston Place A complete hotel, retail, dining and convention complex in the heart of historic Charleston, South Carolina.

Trolley Square This historic, downtown redevelopment Festival Marketplace located in Salt Lake City, Utah, will boast over 100 specialty stores when it opens in late 1988.

World Forum Center The world's most complete conference complex including hotel, recreation, dining and retail facilities opening in 1989 in downtown Philadelphia, Pennsylvania.

Square One An exciting new concept in metro-centre shopping and dining opening in 1989 in sunsational Phoenix, Arizona.

Charleston Festival Marketplace A waterfront extravaganza in the metro-centre of Charleston, South Carolina. Multi-level specialty shopping and dining complex. Opening in 1989.

Aloha Towers A $200 million premiere attraction in Honolulu's exciting cruise ship terminal—Festival Marketplace. Five-Star hotel, historic Hawaiian Museum complex opening in 1990.

Cordish Embry & Associates/Developers
300 WATER STREET
BALTIMORE, MD 21202
(301) 752-5444

Familiar Favorites

You wouldn't go to an afternoon sports event wearing evening dress, neither would you go to your office wearing tennis shorts. You wear the clothes that correspond to the occasion. A store facade is like the clothes you wear, in that it identifies an "event", be it casual, formal, active sports, country, city, young or old. The "event" in this case, is the marketing of products for sale. The store front must be appropriate for the marketing image that the retailer wishes to portray. It is the first impression that the customer receives, and conveys an image, however subliminal, about the quality, style, type of merchandise and service expected inside. If the goods and service do not match the expectation created by the store facade, then however beautiful it may be, The Facade is a failure.

Andre Ruellan, FISP, ASID, President
Design Team/Ruellan

O ld friends well met,—memories from our childhood,—or new visits to old places once seen. These are the old, familiar cliches refurbished and brought up-to-date,—given a new shine —a new vigor—and a new way of saying "hello" to the shopper out there. This is "The World According to Walt Disney"; all the expected and the usual,—freshly painted, primped and polished to make an easily recognized statement. It seems to be so much more "romantic" to shop for food in a "Provincial-type" store, or more "in the mood" to buy the parka and skis in a replica of a Swiss Chalet. Tobacco seems to exude a richer aroma in a Tudor, half-timber structure just as there is a greater sense of adventure in buying safari-type clothes in a "jungle outpost" complete with vines, exotic foliage, rocks and a jeep. These are the Familiar Favorites; the essence of the shop's image reinterpreted in the vocabulary of building materials and design ele-ments,—Up Front—as the store front—an invitation to step into another world or time—another place— another "life" an adventure into the "unknown" but still "known" because the store's facade is constructed of recognizable symbols.

Sometimes, the Familiar Favorites can get kitch and cloying—just too precious or cute and maybe "too much" for the more sophisticated palette, but—for many others—the Bavarian Bakery or the Tower of Pisa Pizza-parlour may be just the right and happy note. In this chapter, we present only a few of what we feel are successful adaptations of the Familiar Favorites —with special emphasis on how they "live next door" to other retail shops in malls—in strip centers—where it is sometimes necessary to "blend"—for the betterment of the community—and yet still not lose their special identity.

Children's World, London, England
Designer: Fitch & Co., London

Sarabeth's Kitchen, Columbus Ave., NY   Design: Grandesign, NY

Horton Toy & Doll, Horton Plaza, San Diego, CA

Charm sells! People do carry their memories with them into the market place and will "shop" where they feel their dreams are being fulfilled. Sarabeth's Kitchen has a new/old, warm, homey and friendly exterior,—from the striped awnings to the multi-mullioned windows and the happy colors. There is a touch of universal-provincial with a flavoring of Americana and a soupcon of the spirit that appeals to Yuppie customers. Horton Toy & Doll brings back visions of the Bavarian Alps—of wood-carver shops—of toy makers who look like Disney's Gepetto—and a time when toys lasted past Christmas morning. A model train puffs along over the signed canopy and disappears into a "tunnel" only to reappear through the opening on the other side. An exterior design with movement! What could spell out children's toys more forcibly than wooden blocks that we all remember. The Patowmack Toy Company's facade is "built" of giant, colorful blocks with display windows worked into the design—and it reaches out to shoppers of all ages by its color, its scale—and its reawakening of thoughts of happy times gone by.

Patowmack Toy Shop, Columbia Mall, Columbia, MD
Developer: The Rouse Co.

Why walk when you can Take a Taxi—and Take a Taxi reaches out to young, trendy misses with its bright white, yellow and black tiled facade and the familiar checkerboard design that ties the outside into the inside in an easy flow. The signage takes up the fun attitude and the open front allows the real taxis inside to become focal displays from the outside. Hickory Farms' red barn front says it all; dairy fresh—cheese and all good things from the farm. The rough wood planking and the double pitched roof are easily recognizable across the many malls in which there are Hickory Farms. Wild Horizons appeals to the man—and woman—who likes to "rough it"—to go rustic—to get "back to nature". The rough, hewn log cabin could have been a stage set for "Call of the Wild"—and you almost expect a friendly grizzley to come up and beg for a peanut butter sandwich. The angled facade takes you away from the glitz and glitter of the mall—under a dark blue sky to a giant tree going up into that "sky". The show window combines the provincial with the merchant's need to show off what's going on inside the wood-lined interior. The store paved floor completes the picture.

Hickory Farms, Columbia Mall, Columbia, MD

Wild Horizons, Horton Plaza, San Diego, CA

Remember "Streamline"—when it meant roaring trains and spiffy designs with long, horizontal lines that suggested stretch and speed? A streamlined train, right out of the 40s could have been the model for Leather Station where it is all aboard for big values in leather accessories. The front is a blend of white laminate, chromed bands and brilliant red enamel,—bent, curved and shaped into the familiar railroad car. The "picture windows" are just right for looking in—as they were originally designed for looking out. Lucky's Diner also brings back memories of American Grafitti—a vision of what Hollywood tells us the innocent 50s were all about. This is today's version of the "hang-out"—the hamburger haunt—the "after-the-date" coffee stop of the past. The facade is designed with long, traveling lines that break out into a big round window with semi-circular ends. The sign completes the Retro fashion.

Leather Station, Horton Plaza, San Diego, CA

Luckys Diner, Woodfield Mall, Schaumberg, IL   Developer: The Taubman Co.

Grills and Lattice-work,—Victoriana and Americana brought into the 20th century with love and memories of another time and another world—of "the good old days". Natures Jewelry comes off a long, lazy porch of an old spreading gingerbread house in middle America of the late 19th century. The long, shallow shop is almost all facade with show windows where there aren't openings into the store. The color scheme is Wedgewood blue and crisp white with brass molding strips, rosettes and lanterns. The details have been contemporized—but the memories linger on. Just like Grandma made it—"home baked"—"from the hearth"—and more of "the good old days". This bakery/coffee shop, Grain D'Or, joins light natural wood with freshly-painted white trim to get its message across. The small window panes and diamond designs go with the neo-classic pediment over the doorway, and the bay window tells a familiar story of days when bread was made of wheat—not chemicals.

Natures Jewelry, Horton Plaza, San Diego, CA

Grain D'Or, San Francisco, CA   Design: Phillip George Assoc., NY

Ducks & Co., Fashion Valley, San Diego, CA

What angled canopies and bowed windows can do for a store's image. Ducks & Co. sells better women's separates and stakes out its South California claim with the creamy stucco facade and the barest of Mission styling. The bow windows—divided into glazed rectangles and capped with a patina-green roof suggests a country cottage heritage where one is relaxed—and the living is easy—so one dresses accordingly. In the same fashion mall, Brady's reaches out to the man who might be accompanying the woman being courted above. The stucco is replaced by a comfortable, manly texture like brick and the set back, arched over double door is decorated with a Victorian-like leaded glass. Though metaphors and periods are mixed, what comes through is a country-gentleman's shop—casual and relaxed.

More New England than Denver, but definitely

Brady's, Fashion Valley, San Diego, CA

A.E. Meek, Stout St., Denver, CO   Design: Engel/Kieding, Denver, CO

designed to say "traditional". The A.E. Meek Co. has an established reputation; its been around serving for some time and wants to let the shopper on the street know it. The crisp and contemporary facade has been "aged" by the brick panels that flank the dark wood doors, and the brass lanterns on the pier. The show windows have been framed in dark metal,—the same as the two slender verticals that break up the stuccoed space between the piers and the period handle on the doors. What is more "masculine" than an Old English shop; half-timbered, and all that was old before Dickens penned his Christmas Carol. The Toggery Shop is heavy woodwork; corbels, panels, mullions, and supports,—the design could be at home in merry olde anywhere. In the midst of pastels and shiny aluminum facades, this store reaches out to the tailored man who wants tradition in his high fashion.

The Toggery Shop, Fashion Valley, San Diego, CA

73

Banana Republic, The Falls, Miami, FL

A study in image and presentation. Banana Republic has been making itself visible in malls and fashion centers across the country,—showing itself as a sophisticated source for easy to wear, traveling clothes and sportswear. When it first "jeeped" its way into view, it made an immediate and lasting impression, but how do you maintain that impetus when you can't cookie-cut your way across the country? So many malls today have definite boundaries—barriers—restrictions on what the store front designer may or may not do. Here we present only four examples of how the Banana Republic has kept its "look" yet maintained peace with developers—and neighbors. Wherever possible—and permitted, the designers have stepped forward with a "native" portico of lashed bamboo—sometimes left

Banana Republic,
Bal Harbour, Miami, FL

bare—sometimes covered with dried palm matting or even corrugated tin. Space allowing and mall management permitting, the familiar jeep makes it on the outside, otherwise it becomes an up front window display fixture. Stones, rocks and boulders,—rough-hewn wood—elephant tusk arches—and live or not so live tropical trees are other easily spotted and remembered elements in a Banana Republic facade. The facade shown lower right is in the new Galleria in Baltimore where all store fronts must be set back behind simple, floor to ceiling glass enclosures. Here too they were able to prevail on the Rouse Corp. and get their "portico" out in front of the glass. The shopper must step inside to enjoy the rest of the jungle fantasy.

Banana Republic, Galleria, Ft. Lauderdale, FL

Banana Republic, Galleria, Baltimore, MD

Rehabs & The Past Remembered

We believe our storefront design should reflect a portion of what is going on from the inside to the outside without giving it all away. Keeping this sense of discovery we feel creates the desire to enter and explore.

Determining how the store is first experienced or viewed is very important. By knowing if it is first seen is from a car, a pedestrian mall or on the street is very important in our philosophy of design. Determining the image the store wants to project to the public is also important in the philosophy of design. Once these concepts are established, our philosophy is to keep the storefront simple without getting too caught up in trendy architecture that gets dated quickly.

We establish the envelope around the client's product and do not let the architecture overwhelm the product. In most cases, our quality of architecture creates an image that truly reflects the product and client, yet still creates enough of an advertisement to the public.

Mark D. Stumer, R.A.
Mojo-Stumer Architects
Great Neck, NY

The originals of the past still stand and speak out to the new shoppers out on the street. The Past is remembered—and with it the graciousness one imagines was part of that bygone day,—the suggestion of Romance—of Tradition—of lasting beauty. In the United States, we have all too often, in the name of Progress, pulled down our past to make way for our future,—forgetting that usually the future is built on the firm foundation of the past—and the things we learned. Recently, it has become "fashionable" and economically feasible to Rehab,—rehabilitate tired, old, oft-time neglected structures into vital new envelopes and retail environments. We are saving our past and making it work with our future. There is something that clings in these new-old buildings that reaches out to the shopper and provides a feeling of comfort—of old-fashioned conveniences—of a more leisurely, less competitive, cut-throat, way-of-life. The rehabs become celebrations; festive places that live again.

In this collection we are presenting some old buildings with new make-up and freshened-up facades; some genuinely old buildings that still function though the uses to which they are put may be "foreign" to the original builder's concepts. Some have been lovingly restored and maybe only minutely altered to provide the right "face" for the new tenant. Sometimes they stand out and away from all the contemporization that has gone on around them, while in other instances they are part of a landmarked area where the venerable buildings are protected from the greediness of realtors and the unkind cuts and patches of insensitive architects or designers. In the midst of all the new, we celebrate the old—and the old that is new again.

The Limited, Madison Ave., NY
Original Architects: McKim, Mead & White, NY
Revision Architects: Beyer, Blinder & Bell, NY

La Ceramica Boutique, Caracas, Venezuela

What it was—it isn't anymore! Here we show some dwellings that were converted into retail spaces and mostly they were rehabbed and revitalized with large, dramatic panels of color. La Ceramica Boutique is actually hidden behind the brilliant splash of red ceramic tiles that pave the exaggerated sweep of roof.

Giuseppe is an up-scale men's tailor and this fifty year old house has taken on a new life thanks to the bold black, white and red color scheme—and the dynamic night-time lighting. Color and light have raised the house out of the doldrum and turned it into a steamship-slick look of the moderne 30s.

Giuseppe, East Hills, NY   Architect: Mojo/Stumer, Great Neck, NY

Cache, Worth Ave., Palm Beach, FL

The Spanish Colonial look is still cherished by many Floridians,—part of the state's heritage—and partly its promise of a Fountain of Youth for the up-scaled shoppers on Worth Avenue in Palm Beach. Cache's facade could just as easily have been the entrance to the Mayor's office—or the Governor of the Province two centuries ago. The Jesuit baroque stone arched opening on the creamy stucco, stepped-forward, facade is topped with terra cotta tiles. The advancing portico creates a pleasant, shadow filled loggia for sun-weary shoppers. In a more intimate mood, Stinchfield has turned this small Spanish influenced arcade that backed up a gracious old "palazzo" into a fashion window by glassing in the area behind the colored, terra-cotta trimmed colonnettes and repeating arches.

Stinchfields, Worth Ave., Palm Beach, FL

Gear, Seventh Ave., Chelsea, NY   Design: Rosenblum/Harb, NY

Three old time New York buildings—one goes back almost 100 years, are presented in their fresh, updated looks. Gear took over a warehouse in Chelsea and opened up their windows to bring the whole retail space into view. The original brick structure becomes the framework for the metal-mullioned, floor-to ceiling windows—finished with decorative, seasonal canvas valances. Beau Brummel, situated in a landmarked, cast iron building stayed honest to the original period but updated the show window and entrance door with clean woodwork that bespeaks of tradition yet complements the new, high fashion menswear. Emo is all new—all glass and metal—and all contemporary. The old three story building was gutted on the inside and simplified on the outside—with a wide expanse of unobstructed glass that allows the three levels of the store visible to the shopper on the street.

Beau Brummel, W. Broadway, Soho, NY   Design: Spitzer & Assoc., NY

Emo, Prince St., Soho, NY   Design: Esposito/Hassman, NY

Optic 2000, Ave. de Tourville, Paris, France

Frette, Bond St., London, England

A pair of continental updated "antiques". Optic 2000 has a simple facade with a slightly arched top outlined with chromed molding. What really makes it unique are the doors; they are decorative "eye-charts" with un-related mirrored letters applied to the clear glass—and the floor to ceiling chromed tube door pulls which serve as handles into this optometrist shop. Frette sits on Bond St.—its new facade put up under a 19th century building. Gray granite provides the architectural proscenium and black lacquered metal is used for the symmetrical presentation windows and the recessed doorway. The brushed steel letters on the neutral stone is dignified—but legible.

Bernard Parris, New York, NY

Ralph Lauren Polo, Madison Ave., NY

Details like they just don't make 'em anymore. Ralph
Lauren Polo is quite comfortably "at home" in the old
landmarked Rhinelander Mansion on Madison Ave.
The ornate, turn-of-the-century, stonework on the
Renaissance Revival structure has been cleaned,
repaired and polished, and what has been added to the
existing facade has been done with taste, tact and
consideration for what was there. The blue awnings
over the windows,—the planters in front of the
windows—and the barrel-vaulted canopy that connects
the curb to the building are all done with restraint but
manage to bring the Polo name up to the shopper.
Right: one of the entrances into the famous Harrod's
Department store in London where tradition reigns
along with the Queen. The red stone facade has been
carefully tended to and kept as lovely and as ornate as
it was when it was built almost 100 years ago. Though
the interior of the store—with the exception, happily, of
the Food Hall, is always changing and keeping up with
the times but the exterior remains proud, elegant and
filled with the richness of its past.

Harrod's, Hans Crescent, London, England

Stephen Sanders & Associates is an architectural design firm that specializes in developing new retail store prototypes and coordinating their implementation into the marketplace.

Working carefully with our clients, we develop concepts and images that reflect and enhance the specific merchandise or services they offer.

The results are exciting environments that reinforce the products, services, and corporate philosophy, thus providing each company with stores that have distinct and relevant identities.

All this is accomplished within the strict constraints of timing and budget that are so critical to the success of each project.

PARTIAL CLIENT LIST

Jaeger Sportswear
John Gerald Jewelers
Record World
Parfumerie Douglas
London Majesty
Saint Laurent Rive Gauche
Courreges
Dana Cote D'Azure
Louis Vuitton
Ascot Jewelers
Harwyn Florsheim
Stadler Florsheim
Parklane Hosiery
Nickels Shoes
Playland Toys
U.S. General Hardware
Card Tec
Athliesure
Athletes Foot
Bonds
Hallmark Cards
Kreeger & Sons
Hempstead China
Frankels
The Shoe Box
La Croissanterie
Cohen Fashion Optical

STEPHEN SANDERS & ASSOCIATES

ARCHITECTURE
INTERIORS
STORE DESIGN

1447 Northern Boulevard
Manhasset, New York 11030
516-365-8106

Fun & Funky

The design of a store's facades, shopfront and windows are fundamental in projecting what the message and personality of the retailer is.

When we are at the stage of designing a shopfront from an architectural point of view—exploring fascia, materials, windows and door configurations and design details, we also simultaneously consider what the central philosophy will be of product presentation in windows.

The shopfront essentially creates the framework for the windows—and in its' overall style, sets the tone for the business. The windows actually sell the product—and represent a changing story—that must keep the customer interested. The two areas must be addressed together if the overall statement of a store from the street—or within a mall is going to be confident and positive enough for a customer to want to cross the threshold and enter the spirit of the store. Essentially, the visual styling of the shopfront should capture the spirit of the retailer.

David Davies
David Davies Assoc.
London, England

"W hen our hearts are young and gay"—we shop more easily and spend more readily. A smiling, happy customer can make the selling-buying process a symbiotic pleasure. In this collection, we approach some facades that more often than not reach out from the building to grab you—shake you and tickle you. Usually the "you" they reach out for are young; young in years and/or in spirit. These store fronts are fun; they are often irreverent and mainly outrageous. Subtlety, sophistication and quality are omitted in this category where the emphasis is on color, shock and sometimes shlock. Some of our examples come from one long, retail street in Los Angeles where this look is expected and even desirable. The cacaphony of vibrating colors and sound blasting out on to the street is "right" for the retailers,—their merchandise—and their targetted market. Since this is a "neighborhood"—they do co-exist in a rather strident form of "harmony". Other examples,—out of "this pond"—make bold statements that appear even bolder when compared to their more genteel and refined neighbors.

In these facades,—the cost of execution is negligible and the greatest expenditure is on a wild imagination combined with plaster—paints and bright, sharp colors. We have included "non-outrageous" facades as well that still reach out for a smile—for acceptance and recognition—and do manage to step out from the surrounding gray-greige, stone stucco and cement sameness. A flat, dull and uninspired building wall suddenly takes on depth and dimension and become a diverting bill-board in an old neighborhood that is looking to "kick up its heels" and be accepted by "the young-at-heart". A building, undergoing renovation, covers itself with a layer of plywood and a happy coat of paint,—puts on a smiling face and becomes a friendly neighbor and a welcome addition to the street rather than a clumsy, cumbersome eye-sore. These are for FUN—so enjoy!

Sam Flax, Westwood, Los Angeles, CA

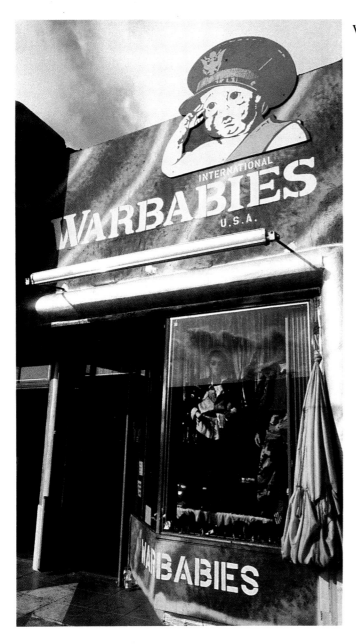

Warbabies, Melrose Ave., Los Angeles, CA

Expo, Melrose Ave., Los Angeles, CA

Though the examples are mostly from Melrose Ave., it doesn't mean that only L.A. can be outrageous—or way-out—or far-out when it comes to getting attention—up front. On the previous page, the Sam Flax art supply store certainly gets attention with the enameled, corrugated metal sculpture that swings, loops, and spirals across the simple white concrete structure. On Melrose Avenue where many of the buildings are left-overs from the 20s and 30s—and haven't had any "tender loving care" in many years,—the new designers and the owners of the new, trendy, off-the-beaten-path shops have taken an approach that relies heavily on paint, plaster, canvas, strong explosive color—imagination and sheer audacity. To be timid or subtle on this street can also mean being overlooked though some of the newer tenants are coming in with a more sophisticated approach to rehabbing and store design. (See Gene Raymond on p. 7). Black seems to be best as a cover-up color and from there—anything goes.

New Kid in Town, Melrose Ave., Los Angeles, CA

New Kid

A New Kid in Town

SALE

7429

DESIGNS BY Tricia Kelly

Claudia's, Horton Plaza, San Diego, CA

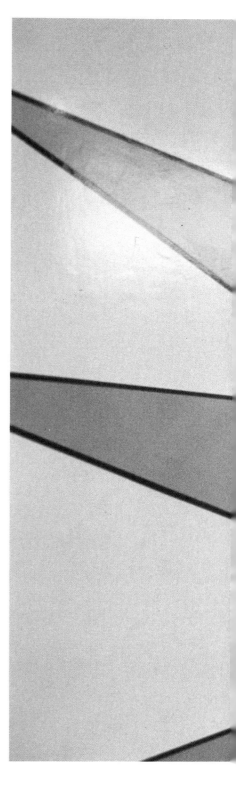

Record's West, Westside Pavillion, Los Angeles, CA

Heroes World, Columbia Mall, Columbia, MD

Excitement seems to be synonymous with fun when it comes to store front design. Talk about explosions—that's what happened in true comic book style in Heroes World (above). It is pop—wham—bop—bam—and the message comes across to every Superman, Spiderman and Batman fan. The dynamic verticals of the burst and the jagged entrance intrigue and involve the young shopper. Records West is Memphisian in its color pizzaz and design elements. The verticals, here, are formed into two ''V's'' that make a striking entrance, and they are complemented by the green zig-zag design that tops the yellow sign board. Claudia's Donut Shop is carefully planned to be off grain—off center and off the straight and narrow. The designers have turned the world askew and filled it with strange angles and odder shapes for a bright, sunny, funny fast-food operation. The facade is only a proscenium—a decorative picture frame for the picture which is open to viewing.

Dudley Do Right's Emporium, Sunset Blvd., Los Angeles, CA   Design: Solo Productions, Laura Solow, Santa Monica, CA

A talented young designer—not afraid to be different, connected with a client who wanted to be different,— and together they created a magical, nonsense world of strange and wonderful birds. The original facade is "lost" under the appliqued material; the birds above and the colorful, "wild" fence that beckons the shopper into the wacky world of Dudley Do Right's Emporium. An unsubtle but amusing "faux" finish finishes off the building. Without benefit of an earth-quake,—a real shaking, crumbling, striking experience takes place in this Nike salesroom. Part of the facade is "cracked and crumbling" and a bright red beam spears its way through the front glass and into the mezzanine within. The white concrete building is eclectically put together with bits and pieces of periods and styles to become a today's look for young, active shoppers searching for a fun experience afoot.

Nike, Westwood, Los Angeles, CA

94

The Gooderham Building, Toronto, Ont., Canada

Tromp l'oeil painting has once again been revived and is succeeding as a method for adding details, decorations and dimension to flat facades. It was popular in the Renaissance period when not everybody could afford arabesques, swags, 3-D cupids and projecting columns and piers. As you travel through Europe you find it reappearing in small cities where the evolving middle class tried to emulate the aristocracy with this art that "deceives the eye". Up in old Toronto, the Gooderham building suddenly comes out from behind its unfurled drapes to reveal the 19th century Romanesque refinement it never had. The Soho Center makes much of its dull, brick side wall with the architectural enrichments painted on—along with the highlights and shadows—and presenting a glory that was usually only reserved for the all important front of the building.

The Soho Center, Prince St., NY

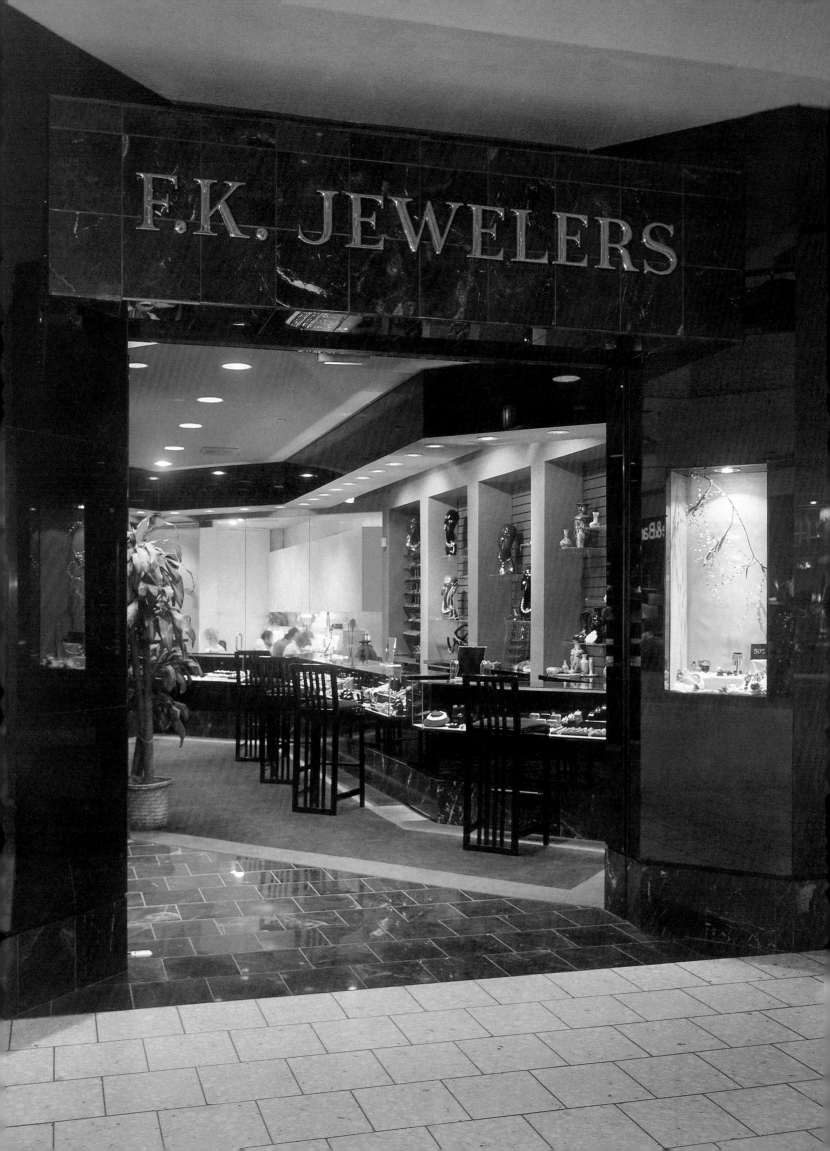

Majestic Marble

A storefront is communication. It is the first and most important opportunity to tell the customer about a store. The front must accurately convey to the customer who you are, and what you sell. A well designed storefront is more than a place to hang a sign and an opening through which the customer enters.

Good design and communication goes beyond the sign. Subtleties in the use of materials, color, graphics and lighting have taken the place of larger signs. The most effective storefront presents a simple, uncluttered message about the store and the product.

The storefront must create drama, excitement and the promise that dreams will be fulfilled. As a proscenium sets the stage for the play, the store front sets the stage for the sale.

John A. Mykebust, AIA, Chief Executive Officer
Myklebust Brockman Associates Inc.
Boston, MA

Marble: cool to the touch but warm to the other senses. It is rich, elegant and aloof; it is smooth, lovely and always interesting. Centuries of time and the interaction of the Earth's elements are compressed in the sleek material, and even when seen at it's whitest or blackest,—there are the subtle markings and patterns created by the veins that travel indiscriminately through the marble and becomes an integral part of it. Some designers require that those veins be book-matched or be diamond-matched, for an even more formal finish in which symmetry reigns supreme, while others may use the marble in tiles and let the basic square shapes make the pattern statement.

Marble is Classic; it is the material of Michelangelo—of the Parthenon—and of the other remembered structures of antiquity. It brings with it—as it sheaths the front of a shop or store,—the essence of permanence—of a "thing of beauty" that remains "a joy forever",—and is strong enough to resist the abrasions of man and time and still appear satiny and lustrous. Marble is Italy and France; it is romantic and "lovely". A Women's boutique can be wrapped in panels of marble and still suggest feminine softness, especially when the designer/architect selects one of the hundreds of face flattering tones of marble that range from the palest whispers of pink streaming through white, to the deeper shades of peach and coral. A Men's shop gains stylishness and sophistication from the rich verdigris and the handsome reddish brown marbles. Jewelry and other "class" merchandise shops may find their identification—their image—in the midnight blacks and pristine whites. As the viewer will see, the designers play their marbles as they see them and as they see their client's personna—with flair and imagination. Marble is forever.

F.K. Jewelers, Woodfield Mall,
Schaumberg, IL The Taubman Co.

Poncet-Faguet, The Esplanade, Palm Beach, FL

Four marble fronted jewelry stores, and each with its own character and image. Though the facing material is the same,—it is handled differently in each facade. Poncet Faguet is quite classic in appearance and the deep green colored marble appears as panels set into the creamy marble background. Brass molding strips and letters highlight the dark surfaces. Also based on classic elements, Graff, however, is contemporary as it sets arches within an arched proscenium, and the vertical panels form an easy curve leading into the shop. The illuminated windows are at eye level and scaled for the merchandise. J.B. Robinson Jewelers and H.T. Stuart are both mall contained shops—and more "open" in their attitude. Both have corner locations and use the angled corners for display space. At Robinson's the glazed area is filled with individual museum cases, while Stuart's has elevated and enclosed it into a shadow box.

Graff, Brompton Rd., London, England

J.B. Robinson's, Town Center, Cobb, GA

H.T. Stuart, Town Center, Boca Raton, FL

Fred The Furrier Design: Mojo/Stumer, Great Neck, NY

Escorpion, Dadeland Mall, Miami, FL

C.D. Peacock, Chicago, IL

Chappell's, Penn Can Mall, Syracuse, NY   Design: Design Associates, Stroudsburg, PA

An impressive rectangle composed of pinkish marble tiles appears to float over the tinted glass and bronze trimmed opening into Escorpion. The same marble tile is laid in the entry as a foyer treatment. The deep gray marble front of Fred the Furrier is relieved by the illuminated stainless steel sign over the door, and on the wall of the return. A wide fascia—also of steel—encompasses and contains the two sides of the facade. Chappell's mall entrance is simple and symmetrical with light gray marble tile facing the front and darker gray tiles—patterned with white—laid on the floor—off the mall. The octagonal planter combines the two grays with a stainless accent band.

Leo Fritzel, Southbridge Mall, Milwaukee, WI

Black marble, lightly veined, is simply and elegantly
used to create a dark proscenium around the light, open
interior of Leo Fritzel. Here too, the dark marble
becomes the "welcoming mat" laid before the carpeted
interior. The marble has been shaped into handsome
moldings that frame the windows and the entrance into

Florsheim's Shoes. Taupe-gray awnings top the
windows while the marble panel over the door wears
the applied bronze letters. It is the gently illuminated
sign and logo in the creamy white entranceway that
distinguishes Smuggler from its neighbors.

Florsheim Shoes,
Bal Harbour, Miami, FL

Smuggler, Town Center, Boca Raton, FL

Black Starr Frost, Galleria, Ft. Lauderdale, FL

"24", Mayfair-in-the-Grove, Coconut Grove, FL

Jessup's is a spectacular in a spectacular mall. The Italian Renaissance striped pattern of black, white and sienna marble has a bold, theatrical presence—and yet, the rich materials maintain the dignity and stature of the jewelry establishment. The arched openings are glazed in with frosted glass panels, and the shiny

Jessup's, Horton Plaza, San Diego, CA
Design: The International Design Group, Toronto, Canada

bright copper panels with molded feature stripping
carry the store's name. The sidewalk—outside—is also
paved in black and white—and thus compliments the
flamboyant pattern on the building. The display
windows are illuminated cubes within a multicubed
filler between the arches.

Courreges, Short Hills, NJ Design: Hashimoto/Plaza, NY

Munson's Chocolates, Trumbull Shopping Park, Trumbull, CT

The international
specialists in
retail store
planning & design

- Analysis of existing facilities, space utilization, productivity and image.
- Conceptual studies for new image projection and improved return on invested space.
- Complete department store planning and interior design services.
- Prototype designs for chain stores.
- Production roll-out of duplicate designs.

DESIGN TEAM • RUELLAN
1133 Broadway #1615
New York, NY 10010-7903 USA

Tel: 212/924-8777
Fax: 212/645-6255

Seven Dimensions of Retail Success

Design International

Research

Design & Development

Architecture

Development Management

Realty

Communications

Store Design

**Cameron Toll Shopping Centre,
Edinburgh, Scotland**

**DI Design
and
Development Consultants, Inc.**

U.S.A. (301) 962-0505
20 South Charles Street
Baltimore, Maryland 21201
Roy Higgs, President

Queen's Quay Terminal, Toronto, Canada

Galtier Plaza, St. Paul, U.S.A.

The Borgata of Scottsdale, Scottsdale, U.S.A.

Belvedere Square, Baltimore, U.S.A.

Canada (416) 595-9598
110 Bond Street
Toronto, Ontario M5B 1X8
Colin C. Stephens, President

U.K. (01) 836-1853
10 Dryden Street
Covent Garden, London WC2E9NA
Paul Mollé, Vice President

Wood,
Wonderful Wood

Architectural literature over the past twenty years has discussed "Architecture As A Sign". This is particularly true of storefronts and is one of the initial considerations in storefront design. To a greater or lesser degree all stores have a "merchandising theme", a message they wish to convey to their customers. This message may say "up-scale, traditional men's store", "family discount clothing", "state-of-the-art video", etc. The design consideration comes in abstracting this message and visually communicating the theme, or the feeling that the theme implies, through architectural materials, detailing, fenestration, entry details, lighting, and signage.

A second consideration is to integrate the storefront into the store design as a whole, drawing the customer into the store. There is no pet formula to accomplish this beyond the necessity to be acutely aware of how you want the store to work and how much you wish to show the store interior from the storefront.

Kay Engel
Engel/Kieding Design Assoc.
Denver, CO

The world of Wood is indeed wondrous. Wood comes in many tints and shades of neutral brown that Man can stain into a palette of unusual colors. Wood is endowed by nature with an infinite variety of patterns and grains that Man can enhance with materials of his own devising. We can see Wood used in its rough bark-state—fresh from the forest—untouched, unvarnished and as natural as the great-outdoors it personifies. Planks of wood can be planed, sanded and lovingly rubbed and waxed till its smooth surface gleams. Wood can be applied in strips —in bands—or in sheets; it can be a riotous design of haphazard patterns or carefully controlled—as veneer panels—and matched to form an harmonious design in which the natural graining becomes a repetitive motif. Wood can be rustic—provincial—the forest primeval; a log cabin, a shack, a country house, an aging barn. Wood can be an elegant 18th century interior; all

smooth, soft and sleek,—fine moldings and carvings— furniture finished. It can be a smart contemporary statement of vertical and/or horizontal lines combined in an arresting design, or the excitement created by diagonal bands rushing to mark out the entrance to a shop. Painted and trimmed, it can be clapboard or shingles and Americana—home and hearth—the "good old days".

In this chapter, we only touch on the versatility of Wood as a facade material. More examples of Wood can be found in the chapter on Familiar Favorites where more "provincial" faces of wood appear. In Neo-Classic Revisited, the reader will find more examples of the finely finished and molding enriched uses of wood in traditional and elegant shops. Lath, strip, sheet or shingle,—log or plank—thick or thin—natural or finished—light or dark—with Wood the possibilities are endless.

Bigsby & Kruthers, Woodfield Mall, Schaumberg, IL

Wood used to face some traditional shops. Bigsby &
Kruthers employs variations of Frank Lloyd Wright's
woodwork paneling on the uprights while Burberry's
adds the mullioned windows to the wood paneled
facade. Ray Pacific is neo-classic in its treatment of the
boiserie; panels with molded frames combined with
enriched crown moldings. Kirk Jewelers appears more
contemporary, by comparison, with its stepped design
and overlapping panels.

Kirk Jewelers, Westside Pavilion, Los Angeles, CA

Burberry's of London, Writer's Square, Denver, CO   Design: Engel/Kieding Design Assoc., Denver, CO   Photo: Ron Johnson, Imageworks

Ray Pacific, Trumbull Shopping Park, Trumbull, CT   Design: Sam Rosenberg, NY

Caren Charles, Coral Square, Coral Springs, FL

Wood in a more contemporary grain. Wood tambour
—many thin wood "pencils" on a heavy canvas
backing—is wrapped around the semi-circular entrance
columns and the squared off lintel above the entrance
into Caren Charles. The quarter-round "awnings" are
part of the architectural design and they are finished in
gray and accented with brass stripes. Ups 'N' Down
also uses the tambour material to create a horizontally
striped entrance. The fine slats are underlined with
wider, colored slats of teal green and terra-cotta. The
widest bands of the accent colors back up the
dimensional letters of the sign. Ann Taylor's facade
consists of a series of contemporary frames that
combine vertical and horizontal slats to make a light-
and-shadow filled presence. The wood merchandising
screens, in the framed windows, continue the linear
pattern play.

Ups 'N' Down, Coral Square, Coral Gables, FL

Ann Taylor, Galleria, Ft. Lauderdale, FL
Design: Charles Broudy & Assoc.,
Philadelphia, PA

115

Crabtree & Evelyn, Promenade, Toronto, Ont., Canada   Design: International Design Group, Toronto, Canada

More traditional wood-faced storefronts where moldings and raised or chamfered edged panels are an important part of the store's look. Blazer is on a busy but old street close by Covent Garden and the facade looks like it could be as old as the building it faces, but the traditional character bespeaks the menswear on view within. Britches, in a mall, tries to capture that same British Traditional flavor with its updated column and pedimented entrance and heavily profiled moldings that serve as bases for the windows. Coffeeworks takes renaissance stonework and reinterprets it in wood planks with brass insets for snap and style—and to accentuate the signage.

Blazer, Longacre St., London, England

Coffeeworks, Willow Brook Mall, NJ   Design: Dorf and Assoc., NY

Britches, Georgetown Mall, Washington, DC

Hudson Trail Outfitters, Ltd., Owings Mills, Baltimore County, MD

Eddie Bauer, Beverly Center, Los Angeles, CA

Brass Boot, Galleria, Ft. Lauderdale, FL   Design: Keith Anderson of Kahler Slater Trophy Engberg, Architects, Milwaukee, WI

Horizontal bands of wood stretch the facade into long, low-slung, structures. The Brass Boot is long, low and elegant with the natural oak "floor" front. The display window follows the same linear feeling and the brass letters stand out. Hudson Trail Outfitters obviously wanted to suggest a log cabin and the rough-hewn logs form the horizontally striped facade with the white "mortar" accentuating the lines. The Eddie Bauer signature sign stretches across the "bowling alley floor" that makes a wide swath on this mall-facing facade. The wood is turned vertically at either side of the entrance. Wood—stained and "aged"—provides the desired "jungle" effect for Banana Republic's appearance in an anything but rustic mall.

Banana Republic, The Esplanade, Palm Springs, FL

119

Heartland Market, Kansas City, MO   Design: Philip George Assoc., NY

Wood plus color. The Heartland Market takes on color as a complement to the grained wood columns that make the vertical statement as they divide the front and side into window bays. Here,—a contemporized "Palladian Motif" with an elevated central arch flanked by two lower arches, and another double arch fills one of the windows below. Brookstone balances the wood and the color in this post-modern design. Neon bands serve as insets between the horizontal bands of the panel over the door and the miniature columns support the "weight" of it all.

Brookstone, Horton Plaza, San Diego, CA

Metal Magic

Our highly competitive retail environment and the rapidly changing consumer has changed forever the way we think about retail buildings, entrances and mall fronts. Today we build on strategies to design buildings and mall fronts that are as distinctive and productive for the retailer as they are convenient and efficient for the customer.

On one hand, our clients need buildings or mall fronts that:
- *Express the nature of business they're in.*
- *Integrate visually, the character of their business.*
- *Suggest simple yet commanding patterns of ingress or egress.*
- *Fore shadows excitement found inside that store.*
- *Provides name recognition.*
- *Erases "threshold barrier" between public and store spaces.*

On the other hand, time-pressed customers are demanding:
- *Views into the store that quickly reveal the merchandise offering.*
- *Clear paths that enable ease of movement through the store.*
- *Service and information at points of ingress such as service desks, coat checks, elevator service, high speed check outs, vehicle drop off lanes and other conveniences.*

As designers of stores for people we must balance out those strategies! Entrances must express business intent of the retailer and make human connections to its customer.

Robert W. Schafer
Schafer Assoc.
Oak Brook, IL

Metal can be cold as steel—hard, sharp, and angular. Metal can be warm and "soft"; —curved and arced,—sensuous and seductive. Metal can be flinty;—gray and structural,—crisp, clean and ultra-contemporary. It can also be the golden glint of a bye-gone era—an enrichment of ornate moldings,—Rococo hardware or a classic name emblazoned in a classic manner. We find metal used sparingly as an accent or a highlight—or to contain and outline glazed areas, but the versatile material can also be used to sheath an exterior in brittle brightness. Metallic finishes include the many laminates that are available and the many finishes and colors that they are available in. It is steel, brass, bronze, copper and aluminum; it is shiny bright or subtley antiqued or rubbed down to a soft glow. It is the sparkle and glitter of angles and faceted corners that pick up the surrounding lights and mirror them back onto the shopper in the mall or out on the street.

The metal covered or accented facade can recall an Art Deco design or a Forties Diner—or be an opulent Baroque frame—a setting for a jewel of a shop. In strips or bands—in wide sheets—, metal lends and bends itself to the designer's needs. Metal can be used to contain an illuminated sign or make a swash of fascia that can underscore or point up the store's name. If the reader follows up with a look back to chapter *#11*, he or she will find metal pipes, rods and tubes worked into structural designs that frame the shop's entrance. Indeed, Metals can be magical is making Up Front statements.

British Home Stores, Bexleyheath, England
Design: McColl, London, England
Photo: Michael Nicholson

Two store fronts where the emphasis is on the horizontal,—but there the resemblance ends. The British Home Store's mall entrance is all aglow and a-glitter with shiny copper strips racing across the front—over the illuminated sign. The same excitement continues on the paneled ceiling where the metal catches and reflects what light it can. Luciano's subtley brushed metal front is gently conceived to evoke memories of sophisticated art deco structures. The horizontal bands are rounded tubes—one atop the next—in a rhythmic pattern. The sign over the double glass doors is blue tinted glass with brass letters and molding strips applied. The facade "sits" on a course of black marble with marble tiled floor to delineate the entrance.

Luciano, Dadeland Mall, Miami, FL
Design: Echeverria Design International,
Miami, FL

124

Fine Design, St. Louis Union Station, St. Louis, MO

Metal dividers and delineations. Blazer becomes a semi-circular retreat off Bond St. and presents a gazebo-like countenance. The vertical lines that divide the windows continue up to become the converging lines in the tent top. In keeping with its historic setting, Fine Goods repeats the arches and the structural feeling of the old, now new, Union Station. The circle over the door fills the arch and frames the simply stated sign. The Limited simulates a contemporary greenhouse in copper and glass as the metal bands define and divide the windows into individual viewing areas. Executive Accoutrements makes a sophisticated pitch by combining brushed, steely gray with sparkling glints of brass to promote expensive "toys".

126

Blazer, Bond St., London, England

The Limited, Coral Square, Coral Gables, FL

Executive Accoutrements   Design: Richardson Smith, Inc., Worthington, OH

Fred the Furrier,
Garden City, NY
Design: Mojo/Stumer
Great Neck, NY

Exit Shop, The Falls, So. Miami, FL

Exit Shop, Town Center, Boca Raton, FL

Sheets of brushed metal take on curves to create sensuous movement into the store. The Exit Shops make two entering statements. Above: a series of sweeping arcs that lead the shopper to the wide central opening. Note the effective changes in the glazed areas of the bowed segments as they approach the center. Below: a contemporary wrap-around, off-centered curve under a horizontally defined fascia.

M.J. Carroll, Trumbull Shopping Park, Trumbull, CT   Design: Jon Greenberg Assoc., Berkley, MI

CPI Photo, Fairlane Mall, Dearborn, MI   The Taubman Co.

More variations on horizontal bands in metal. The M.J. Carroll facade wraps around a corner in an easy curve which is accentuated by the tiers of bands inset with shiny, contrasting metal strips. The fascia of CPI Photo Finish curves down from the mall ceiling and then reverses direction to sweep down to the back wall of the store interior in a graceful S profile.

The Custom Shop, Galleria, Ft. Lauderdale, FL

Neon: Glimmer & Glow

Within the shopping mall environment the storefront is possibly the most important single design element. It is the retailer's first opportunity to stop the people and entice them into the store; once over the threshold it is up to the ambiance and merchandise to do the rest.

More and more the mall criteria is having a substantial impact upon the design. However, as designers, we must resolve this and apply our talents more carefully.

Currently there is an expansion in special finishes available to the designer, particularly with the new marble conglomerates now being developed. Although relatively expensive they are generally thinner than the more traditional marbles and therefore easier to install. They are also more readily available.

Another element which can increase the store image is in the application of company logos. Malls are more flexible in their attitude to neon, comfortable that it doesn't have to appear cheap or gaudy and a whole range of effects are open to us. Low voltage lighting is another major element which is becoming widely accepted and, more readily available at affordable cost.

The storefront design should attract attention but, above all, set the tone for what is to come once inside; they should never offer a false promise. They should represent totally the concept of the store from ambiance through service, merchandise and longevity.

David Wales,
Vice President/Design Director: Specialty Retail
Walker Group/CNI
New York, NY

W hen the Lord said—"Let There Be Light",—He more than separated day from night and lit up the Firmament. He created the First Commandment for Retailers and Architects. Light is what separates night from day— and one store from another in a mall—in a strip center —on a trafficed street. Light is what reaches out from the "darkness" to say—"Here I am". It is the warm and welcoming beacon that leads the rudderless shopper towards a safe, bright, spending "port".

Until recently, Neon was considered tawdry, schlock,—passe. But, in this time, Neon has been rediscovered as a colorful and color-filled art form and signing device; a technique that not only provides the welcoming light, but plays up fanciful designs and motifs. It provides the glitter, glow and sometimes even the glitz that the Retailer wants and needs to announce his wares—his image—and, very important,—his location.

In this cahpter, we review the light, bright, shimmer and shine of Neon—and Light, in general, as an integral part of the store's facade. As you will see, Light is often the major design element of a store front especially when the front is just a yawning opening with little architecture surrounding it. Neon signs have grown up and become part of the respected store architect's vernacular and as David Wales, V.P./Design Director at Walker Group/CNI says: "Now that the Malls are more flexible in their attitude to Neon,— comfortable that it doesn't have to appear cheap or gaudy,—a whole range of effects are open to us which were previously unacceptable".

Record World, Roosevelt Field, Garden City, NY
Design: Steven Sanders & Assoc., Manhasset, NY

Bloomies Express, J.F.K. Airport, Queens, NY Design: Fitzpatrick Design, NY

Traveling Light travels with the light of the neon cancel marks across the logo. The bright red bands are picked up and reflected in the glass and the polished metal bands of the facade. Bloomies Express' sign is neon and it sets the white ceiling of the airport terminal aglow with hot color. That same sizzling glow is evident in Record World on the previous page.

Traveling Light, Westside Pavilion, Los Angeles, CA
Design: Carr Assoc., Los Angeles, CA

Animation Station, Westside Pavilion, Los Angeles, CA

Framed in Neon. The funneling tunnel entrance into Animation Station is enhanced by the rainbow of neon arches that define the circular opening. Sparkle Plenty has a star shaped doorway delineated in pink and blue. In the dark mall, the sign and stars are super visible. Waxie Maxie's Record shop takes on the look of a 40s or 50s Juke Box as the red, yellow and blue neon tubes frame the front. Even Koala Blue's chaste rectangular doorway gets a special play from the neon striping—and the logo over the window.

Koala Blue, Westside Pavilion, Los Angeles, CA

138

Sparkle Plenty, Dadeland Mall, Miami, FL

Waxie Maxie, Potomac Mills, Prince William County, VA

Athena, Maidstone, England   Design: Isherwood Company, London, England

Athena, Gateshead, England   Design: Isherwood Company, London, England

Miso Miso Miso, Royal Bank, Toronto, Ont., Canada

Located throughout England, the Athena stationery and book selling shops are easily identified by the glow of the Athena sign—either executed in neon or illuminated from within. The same sort of design is evident in Miso Miso Miso where two neon signs are separated by a plastic one—back lit to stand away from the fascia. The Caroll store's sign dominates the simple white front and also combines neon tubing and the back glow for effective signage.

Caroll, Eaton Centre, Toronto, Ont., Canada

141

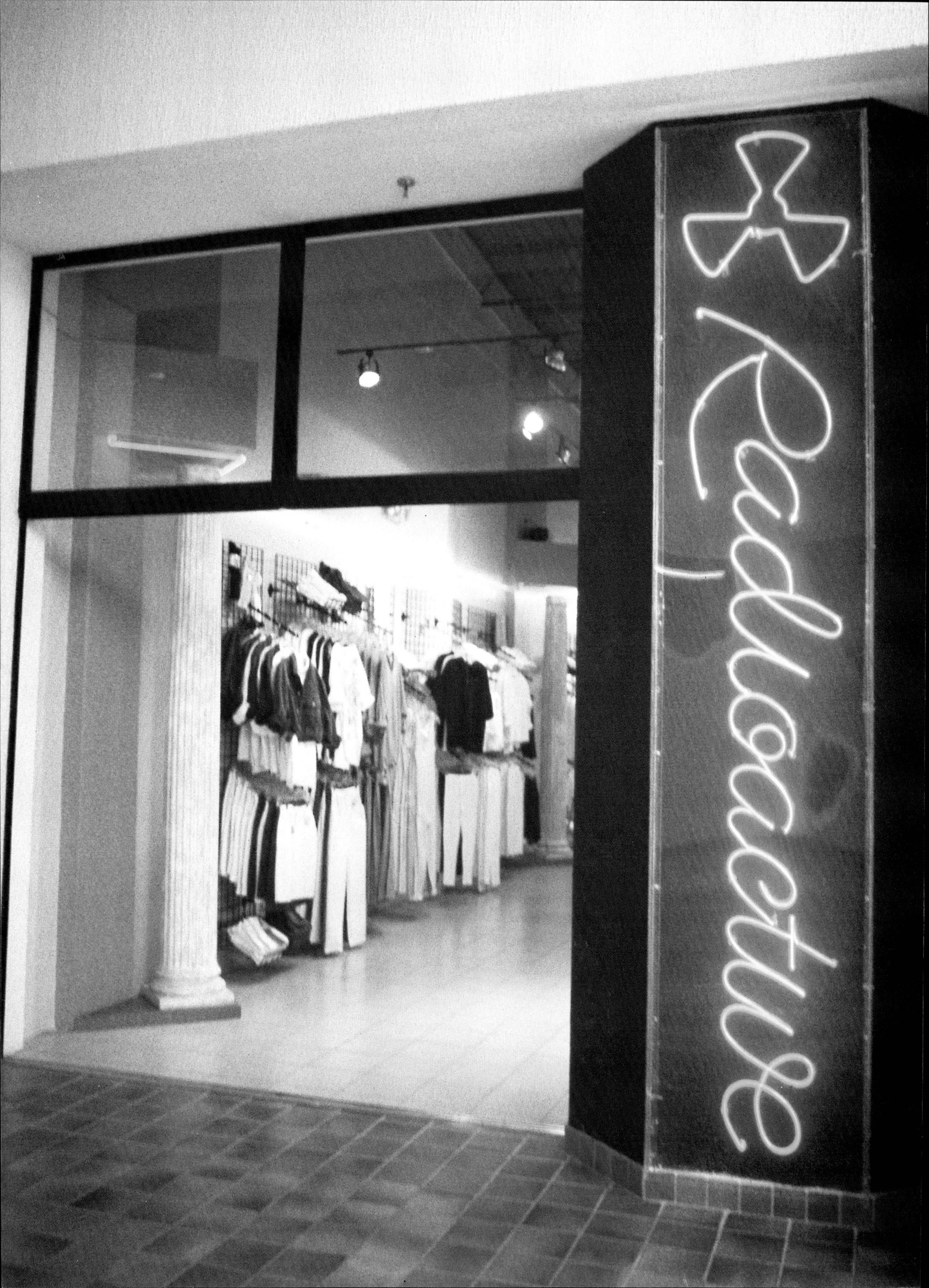
Radioactive

Saturdays, Westside Pavilion, Los Angeles, CA

Saturdays reverses the trend and puts its neon sign below—across the bottom of the window and continues the design with bands that shimmer their way around the corner—and up. The neon path leads to the door. Radioactive turns its signage on end and provides a cool gleam as part of its facade. Inside the store,—the blue neon tube runs along the wall, over the merchandise. Second Sole has a stepped up facade of ceramic tiles with red neon tubes outlining the unusual window. A neon sign stands up, out and away from the tiled surface over the front door—and the main window.

Second Sole, Horton Plaza, San Diego, CA

Radioactive, Town Center, Boca Raton, FL

Burdines, Boynton Beach Mall, Boynton Beach, FL   Design: Walker Group/CNI, NY

Kentucky, Rue Messina, Nice, France

MotoPhoto, Dayton Mall, Dayton, OH   Design: Design Forum, Dayton, OH

In Nice—a way-out shop called Kentucky brings them in with its multi-colored, retro-style, neon sign that is also indebted to some Juke box for its conception. Burdine's new facade reinforces its Florida Store image —and the pink palm tree and sweep of blushing wave below gets the message across. MotoPhoto Image Center manages to make an impression with its dynamic, colorful signage on the fascia.

Sigs, Signs & Sculpture

Good retail design, practicalities apart, is the assembly of a number of "symbols" which in their aggregate send coded signals to tuned in consumer groups. Different symbol collections talk to different customers. In this targeting, the storefront is the beacon.

What are these storefront symbols? The name, the entrance, the windows, the materials, etc. are some of these. How the retailer treats these elements in design terms, will give him what I call "street credibility"! Mishandled and the shopfront will fail to support either the merchandising or positioning effort, let alone the corporate culture.

So, entrances that are important, obvious and bright to attract customers like moths: a fascia where the name is clear and distinctive, materials that are durable and appropriate to differing climatic and locational circumstances: windows that are not art but tell merchandise stories—plat de jour to the a la carte opportunities in the store.

Differentiation by design is the goal.

Rodney Fitch, President
Fitch & Co.
London, England

In bygone days,—before society attempted mass literacy,—communication with the masses was through graphic designs either two or three dimensional. The signs that hung in front of retail stores were often fanciful executions of the symbol or symbols that best represented the merchandise or service rendered within. We have become more literate —more sophisticated, and yet, it seems we still respond more readily to the graphic symbols than the written word. As international travel increases and so many countries, including our own, become more like Babel, and one hears many tongues spoken at once in the marketplace,—the definite and definitive sign becomes even more important to the Retailer. It isn't even what it says—but how it is said that matters. The visual imprint—the sig or logo—or the sculptural effect is easier to "read" and makes a more lasting impression.

Even if it is only the representation of the store's name, it too must be presented as a complete visual entity—rather than a number of letters organized to spell out that identity. The impact depends upon the type of letter used—the thinness or thickness of the strokes—the positioning or juxtapositioning of the individual letters. The Tiffany script differs from the Saks Fifth Ave. sig—just as they are both at variance with the free "scrawl" of Lord & Taylor. What the shopper sees is that sig—or the logo—that immediately translates into a name—an image—a perception of who and what lies beyond that opening.

In this chapter and in Open To Viewing where the architectural elements are almost non-existent, the sign becomes the major element for recognition. Here are some successful signs—sigs—and sculptural effects.

Top Man, Waterford, England   Design: McColl, London

Burton, London, England   Design: Fitch & Co., London, England

Principles, Oxford St., London, England   Design: McColl, London

Three British entries that are far from traditional and reserved. In each case, the designers created new logos —new color schemes—and dramatic opening statements for the shops. Since each store is part of a chain, the signature becomes easily recognizable and the architects have sculpted their storefronts into exciting sweeps that break out from the straight and "square".

Apropos, Fashion Valley, San Diego, CA

Apropos' facade is a piece of sculpture; a dimension stuccoed slab with carefully removed bits and pieces that become the display windows. The cut-outs vary in shape and size and in relation to the eye-level. The long vertical windows feature dresses while accessories are fitted into the horizontal ones. Hamilton's facade has crumbled away leaving only a pristine sign—and the scalloped edge of an awning. Over the entrance to Pompano Square, metal waves support the pink and blue sign of seashells and more waves. The Athens Kwik Frame shop takes on a dimensional look as forms are applied over forms to become a 3-D collage.

Hamilton, Weyburn Ave., Westwood, Los Angeles, CA

150

Pompano Square, Pompano Beach, FL   Design: Walker Group/CNI, NY

Athena, Oxford, England
Design: Isherwood Company, London

Potomac Mills, Prince William County, VA

Hats, Horton Plaza, San Diego, CA

Claudia's, Horton Plaza, San Diego, CA

Sculpted Signs; where scale and dimension count. Left: three of the many large elements that appear throughout Potomac Mills—a value-oriented mall that gains an up-scale look by using these imaginative, well-designed signs over otherwise utilitarian facades. Right: two of the unique store fronts in Horton Plaza that make much of their sculpted signs and logos—that become the memorable part of their store fronts.

Country San Francisco, San Francisco, CA   Design: Ace Architects, Oakland, CA

A minute shop with a mighty attractive logo-sign that really d-r-a-w-s them in. It's magnetic at Magnet, P.I.—a clever little shop that stocks thousands of magnets. The designers have defined the shop with brightly colored doors and white framed windows, but it is the sign out front that is the store's main attraction. Country San Francisco is a simple, wooden structure that boasts an oversized steer stomping over the doorway. Z Gallerie takes on a high-tech look with the mesh and metal sculpted frieze that wraps around over the stuccoed facade—and carries the signage.

Z Gallerie, Horton Plaza, San Diego, CA

B-Club, Crossgates Mall, Albany, NY

Athletes Foot, Galleria, Ft. Lauderdale, FL

Debenham's, Oxford St., London, England
Design: Fitch & Co., London

The new Debenhams that stands on Oxford Street is where the old Debenham's stood—and that's all. The architects and designers changed it all,—inside and out—and the new Debenham's logo and coloration gets a play out in the street on the heroic arches that indicate the store entrances. A formal topiary garden is planted on the marquee that cantilevers out from the building providing cover for the shoppers below.

Zigs & Zags

The importance of designing an effective store front is more than just creating a good first impression. The impression must affirm the store's image, merchandise, attitude in many ways. It should tell the customer what to expect while at the same time encouraging and stimulating her to enter and find out.

The store front is a visual stopper as well as a practical expedient for traffic control and direction. It should be easily recognizable and distinguishable from its neighbors. Materials used are of vital importance, their quality, cultural associations, relationships all affecting the total picture. Marble, porcelain ceramic tile, woods all have visual connotations to the viewer. Glass and mirror bring glitter and reflection while affording inviting and helpful views of the store interiors.

Design of the facade and interior should interrelate in order to establish a comfortable flow, without significant breaks in design.

The store front should be versatile enough to collaborate visually with seasonal merchandising requirements.

But above all, it should be right for that particular store. As presentation at a very significant level, its value cannot be overestimated.

Ken H. Pfeiffer, President
Pfeiffer & Miro Associates
New York, NY

Sometimes it takes more than an opening to entice a shopper in. It may require more finesse—more subtlety—to direct the shopper to the entrance and to persuade her to step over the threshold —and culminate a tour that began outside the store. In order to accomplish this gentle push—to conduct and direct the shopper, the architect/store designer may zig and zag,—use angles and diagonal lines to create that desire to enter. Instead of a long, flat expanse of glass—or a non-holding-back gaping opening, the viewer is treated to individual setbacks or set-forths,—angled cuts that create specialized show case display areas that can heighten the anticipation of finding the entrance which leads to the merchandise that has just been sampled. Museum cases or show cases in echelon can do the same thing where there is no glassed in areas. The zigs and zags may also suggest the traffic plan the shopper will find inside; diagonal cuts and corners rather than "cut & dry" rectangular grids. The angled facade also suggests a thrust—a movement into the store where the architectural elements are limited and the glass panels and glass enclosed projections or step-backs must do the "sweeping".

So, let's turn some corners—cut some angles—as we zig and zag into this collection of angled openings.

Korakuen-Shopin Tokyo
Beverly Center, Los Angeles, CA

Brass Boot, Bal Harbour, Miami, FL
Design: Keith Anderson of
Kahler Slater Trophy Engberg,
Architects, Milwaukee, WI

Tourneau, Bal Harbour, Miami, FL

Alexio (formerly Robert Phillips), Beverly Center, Los Angeles, CA   Design: Patrick Maddox and Co., San Diego, CA

Each step back—each angle creates a new viewing experience. Alexio (formerly Robert Phillips) is faced with black marble and the flesh colored column that marks the corner is used as a recurring theme inside the store. The set-back windows—as in the Tourneau shop—provide the shopper with special, focalized viewing.

161

Executive Accoutrements   Design: Richardson Smith & Co., Worthington, OH

"We have trouble with the term 'Storefronts'. It brings to mind images of Dodge City during the 'Gunsmoke' days when grandiose facades were stuck on the front of humble structures in order to make them appear to be something that they are not; a harlequin mask. Our approach is to focus on the store and develop an entry which reflects the identity of the whole. We want to create a face in keeping with the gestalt; a face with character, a window to the soul—not just another pretty face. Our goal is to create a path which carries shoppers unselfconsciously to the interior. We want them to feel allured."
Howard Hinterthuer, Dir. of Public Relations
Kubala-Washatko, Architects
Cedarburg, WI

August Max, Boynton Beach Mall, Boynton Beach, FL

Johnson & Murphy, Westside Pavilion, Los Angeles, CA

Papillon, Short Hills Mall, NJ

Peoples, Montreal, Quebec, Canada
Design: International Design Group, Toronto, Canada

Diva: Franklin Park Mall, Toledo, OH
Design: Jon Greenberg Assoc., Berkley, MI

Three wide-open, storefronts that are zigged and zagged
to direct the shopper into the store. Jess has lots of
glass while Diva and Peoples have none. The latter two
have fixtures—on an angle—to create the desired
directional flow into the merchandised space.

Jess, Beverly Center, Los Angeles, CA   165

Lenscrafters, Rose Park Mall, Pittsburgh, PA   Design: Space Design International, Cincinnati, OH

Lenscrafters bold blue overhead fascia is supported on angled wood panels and the supporting column, center, is sheathed in wood. A V-shaped counter juts out into the mall and forms a directional entrance. The Ciro shop has a similar motif and the wedge-shaped window thrusts forward from the shop. The Ciro sign is not only centered above, but makes a graphic imprint on the side wall of the shop—and is part of the facade design. The Optic Fashion Center is small and angled to get maximum visibility from three sides of the mall.

Optic Fashion Center, Beverly Center, Los Angeles, CA

Unifying Elements

*In the gentrification of the regional shopping center, we are attracting an
educated and more sophisticated shopper. Likewise the appearance and impact
of storefront designs now have paramount importance.*

*The image of the store must make an impression on the customer in two to
eight seconds. The store facade must create an impression and personality that
is indelible and unique to the product line and target customer. Even the lowest
price point stores now understand that design and visual presentation are vital
to their success.*

*The lease line presentation in a regional center can no longer be just an
open storefront with a plastic laminate sign band, but must evoke an emotional
response from its target customer by orchestrating all the design elements into a
perfect envelope. As a developer, The Taubman Company is interested in the
impact of the storefront; yet, the Design Staff is also interested in maintaining a
cohesiveness by repeating the design theme of the storefront throughout the
interior.*

*We understand the regional centers' tenant needs, and at the same time
challenge the retailers to the highest standards of design.*

Larry Ebel
Sr. Designer/Asst. Dir. of Store Planning & Design
The Taubman Co., Bloomingfield Hills, IL

Getting it all together! In this chapter we will
show various ways of "pulling together"—
making a common statement in an
uncommon way that still benefits each of the
individuals involved. This chapter could have been
subtitled—"In Union there is strength"—or "United
we stand" against the opposition. The unifying element
can be a single stretch of facade—with careful attention
given to the individuals assembled below—that makes a
statement in a strip center standing alongside a well
traveled road, or it can be a far reaching expanse of
individual, but same, awnings extending out from a
cluster of buildings (similar or dissimilar) that unifies a
group of retailers into one, strong selling voice. We will
present a single shopping mall where the overall effect
triumphed in creating an homogenous sense of
space—and yet each retailer could, within the

parameters set by management, create its own special
look—its own special appeal—and still reinforce the
overall gracious feeling of the mall. Here too we see
Familiar Favorites and Neo-classic Revisited,—blended
to conform with the particular geographic area—to the
customers—and the customers "traditional
environment and way of life".

The unifying facade gets the group together for
impact—to make a statement that says "here,—in one
cluster—is convenience, comfort, and whatever you,
the customer, wants". It avoids the confusion and
blustering signage,—eye-sore exposures that not only
point up the bad taste of the particular retailer but does
affect the neighbors with the same blight of bad taste.
It guarantees a single face—a single voice that calls out
to a demographic segment—"we are here to serve you
and supply you with what you want".

Mendelsohn's, St. Francis Hotel, San Francisco, CA

Awnings can collect a group of assorted openings and
present them as a coherent and logical entity. They
become the "fascia"—the wide, horizontal band that
contains the windows and entrances below.
Mendelsohn's puts on a distinctive front with these
elongated, elegantly striped awnings that set this shop
apart from the hotel of which it is a part. Hardly a strip
center—more like an exclusive, upper-upper mini-mall,
The Harborside in Roslyn presents a unified
appearance architecturally and stylistically,—that seems
to be working for the benefit of the tenants—as well as
the shoppers.

Harbourview Shoppers, Roslyn, NY
Design: RAL Design, Hempstead, NY

170

Godiva, Charleston Pl., Charleston, SC

All of these shops are part of the Taubman Company's Charleston Place in Charleston, SC. Each of the shops was required to conform to the Antebellum style that was established for the enclosed mall; to find their architectural expressions in the 18th and 19th century American heritage—and in the structures that still stand in Charleston. Each store's facade is different and each facade also adheres to the overall look of the mall. It is a gracious and gentle shopping experience—an extension of the city in which it is found. There are more examples on the following pages.

Designs: Wayne E. Visbeen, Design Coordinator
Larry Ebel, Senior Designer, Asst. Dir. of Store Design

Kenneth Jay Lane, Charleston Pl., Charleston, SC

Elson's, Charleston Pl., Charleston, SC

"A store's invitation to the consumer is the storefront. It attracts the customers attention by sending an instant set of signals to welcome the customer and identify the merchandising strategies within.

It is the architecture which first conveys the message which the customer perceives as trendy—friendly—elegant—sleek—Italian or conservative. This perception and customer recognition are reinforced by colors, finishes, graphics—and the merchandise presentation which can be seen as an integral part of the storefront. The storefront should,—from all parts—reflect the feeling of the whole."
Liz Buxton, Material/Design Director
Tucci, Segrete & Rosen, NY

The Gap, Charleston Pl., Charleston, SC   Gucci, Charleston Pl., Charleston, SC

Open to View

The wider the doorway, the wider the welcome. The store throws its arms wide and invites the shopper inside, right? Not necessarily. While extending its invitation, the entrance should also be sending clear signals about merchandise selection. If it's well and cleverly designed, the entrance will welcome primarily the market segment most likely to buy. For example, in a mall setting, a wide open entrance, one that requires little effort to cross the threshold, often suggests volume sales and an emphasis on price, not quality. A narrower, more exclusive looking entrance, especially one that requires the effort of opening a door, usually suggests somewhat upscale merchandise with emphasis on quality. The ideal entrance will so thoroughly reflect the store's personality that targeted shoppers will sense "at homeness" the second they step inside.

Lee Carpenter, President
Design Forum, Dayton, OH

"What you see is what we've got". No surprises—no subtlety—no suspense. A wide-open, yawning expanse that reveals all, puts the whole retail operation on display and makes all the displays count. Often, in malls, it is one gaping opening after another and the only place for one's individuality,—for image projection,—for a one-of-a-kind statement is in the signage above the opening. The fascia, over the glass enclosure is the place to say it all, plus the treatment within the glassed-in areas besides the entrance—if there are any such spaces. Working within the mall developer's design restrictions is challenging and we have collected some effective solutions that have still managed to make Up Front statements while still maintaining a "neighborly" attitude. The material that faces the fascia—the signage and its illumination—the color; they are all involved in creating a successful opening. And, at eye-level, the up front treatment reinforces the message that was first "read" overhead—and from across the mall. The use of displays or fixtures or graphics to invite the shopper in—to possibly add some element of surprise or attraction under almost impossible conditions (and restrictions)—they make the difference and help separate one opening from the next. Even the transparent and seemingly "invisible" glass panels that may front the store can, in the hands of a talented architect/ designer become effective design elements that add up to a special "look". The glass may zig and zag (see Chapter #14) or it may curve, swoop and wrap around. The glass panels can add luster,—twinkle with reflected lights—or just subtley provide the directional flow that will sweep the shopper off the aisle in through the entrance to the store beyond.

All these selections share in common their total exposure—their total "open-to-viewing" store fronts where, with a minimum of materials and places to use those materials, they have to announce who and what they are. What they have to sell is right out there—in the open—for all to see.

Tommy Hilfiger, Columbus Ave., NY
Design: Robert Young Assoc., Alexandria, VA

Crowley's, Tel-12 Mall, Southfield, MI   Design: Jon Greenberg Assoc., Berkley, MI

Spire, Woodfield Mall, Schaumberg, IL

Le Chateau, Woodfield Mall, Schaumberg, IL

Crowley's opening statement is a vast expanse of glass—zigging and zagging across the expanse and presenting an extensive view into the store's interior. Up front,—on elevated platforms, outlined in bee lights, the mannequins are shown under well placed spots. The entrance is faced in gray stone and the illuminated sign reaches out from the semi-darkness. Le Chateau has little facade to hide behind and so it brings the show up front—also on elevated stages—to display the featured merchandise.

Etage, University Square, Tampa, FL   Design: Neidermaier Design, Chicago, IL

The Jewel Box is a box with an open side and a symmetrical layout that invites the shopper into the limited space. The mixture of rich materials and the sparkle of glass and mirror combine to create the "jewel-like" setting. Parisian's mall entrance is inviting and the post and lintel elements that serve as display windows are also aisle liners and architectural focal points on the floor. They repeat the round columns and partial lintels that support the Parisian sign.

Parisian, Riverchase, Hoover, AL   Design: Schafer Assoc., Oak Brook, IL

The Jewel Box, St. Louis Station, St. Louis, MO   Design: Kubala-Washatko, Architects, Cedarberg, WI   Photo: Mark Heffron

Mourette, Promenade, Singapore

Casual Corner, Beverly Center, Los Angeles, CA

Fizzazz, Atlanta, GA   Design: Robert Young Assoc., Alexandria, VA

Fizzazz moves off Main Street into the mall and brings the sparkling effervescence of Coca Cola with it. Under the bubble sign—what you see is what they've got. The designers bring the ladders—the vertical merchandising and clothes-on-a-tray concept to this shop. Casual Corner in its "new" appearances is all glass—all open and all on show. In Mourette—you are only a glass away from the merchandise.

DONALD BRUCE

Donald Bruce, Worth Ave., Palm Beach, FL
Design: Echeverria Design International, Miami, FL

Politix, Weyburn Ave., Westwood, Los Angeles, CA
Design: Fadi Shabshab of Garney Design Inc.,
Los Angeles, CA

Three stores—on Main Street—facing the racing traffic
and trying to stop the shopper. Donald Bruce's clientele
doesn't run; in Palm Beach one strolls—stops to peruse
—to consider. This glazed front invites the shopper to
look in and see the wall displayed merchandise.
Politix—in Westwood where the college students are—
where they study the fashion scene—is opened up and
fully lit. On Columbus Ave., in N.Y.C., Think Big has
to make a big statement for its overscaled merchandise
in its underscaled shop. The look-in facade turns the
entire store into a display set-up—and manages to make
a little into a lot.

Think Big, Columbus Ave., NY
Design: Grandesign, NY

185

Alfred Sung, Short Hills Mall, NJ

The Parisian, Riverchase, Hoover, AL Design: Schafer Assoc., Oak Brook, IL

Meis, Village Mall, Danville, IL   Design: Richard Roeder Assoc., Houston, TX

The Parisian's soaring glass tower glows in the evening light and beckons to shoppers out in the parking lot—and on the road. As one approaches, the whole store seems to come out to greet the shopper. Alfred Sung's glazed facade is divided between display area and entrance. Set back in the presentation portion, a dividing wall provides greater lighting and display opportunities—without affecting the open-to-enter feeling. The Meis department store offers no barriers—only an open invitation.

You are invited to join some of the best creative minds in store planning...

RETAIL REPORTING BUREAU 101 Fifth Avenue New York, New York 10003

MACY'S, Herald Square, New York — Neat and tailored, the working women's favorites are gathered together in this important shop on Macy's Third Floor. The classic nature of the merchandise is brought a colorful and exciting element with the ethnic appeal. Richly neutral color on all surfaces and beamed ceiling work together creating an appealing impression and a perfect place for a variety of merchandise.
81-272S

SUITS/COORDINATES

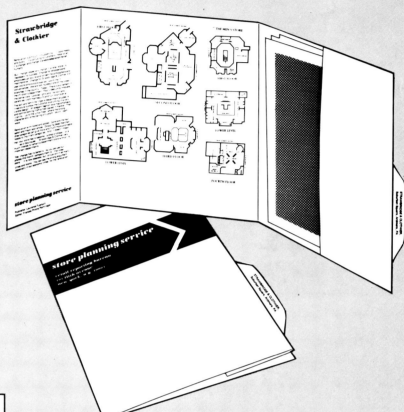

RETAIL REPORTING BUREAU 101 Fifth Avenue New York, New York 10003

ANN TAYLOR
The Court at King of Prussia, PA
Architect: Charles E. Brody & Associates., Phil. PA
Contractor: Ford Building, Inc., 82-179
Ivar Kasaks, N.Y.,N.Y.
Visual Pres. Dir.:Sonny Jaen

Sleek, inviting lines draw us into Ann Taylor. Architecture flows easily from space to space. Rich wood floor, accent ceiling, walls and fixtures follow suit, creating an arrangement to enhance customer traffic flow.
82-179
COPYRIGHT©

There's never been a publication like Store Planning Service. It's a unique publication concerned solely with keeping professionals like you up to date with new store design. By subscribing to Store Planning Service you receive 30 8x10 full color photos per month showing new merchandising concepts — the most recent stores, new installations and rehabs. You'll see new trends and directions as they're developing...the latest techniques — new materials, fixtures, lighting, interior design, visual merchandising and display. Subscribe to Store Planning Service at the rate of $45.00 per month plus postage.

Our Guarantee: If you feel Store Planning Service does not live up to your expectations you can cancel at any time for any reason. For overseas subscription write for the agent in your area.

"Make your selling space into a sparkling selling environment."

Subscribe today, call toll free 800-251-4545 or write:

Retail Reporting Bureau 101 Fifth Ave New York, N.Y. 10003 212•255-9595

STORES OF THE YEAR
BOOK 4

A Pictorial Report on Store Interiors

STORES OF THE YEAR/Book 4 is a Book of Discoveries. It is about stores—large and small—and very small—that are unique, special, different and exciting. These stores feature designs that stimulate the shopper—and sales. Some are basically "traditional" but with a new quality—a new use of familiar materials or unfamiliar materials shaped to classic forms. Other shops are bright, sparkling, innovations —full of fresh vitality and a joie de vivre.

In this Book of Discoveries—over **250 photos from over 60 stores are reproduced in full color**—you will find experimental design concepts side by side with adaptations of 18th Century motifs—Art Deco derivatives and post Post-Modernism. The fixturing, like the decor, goes from "safe" to audacious, and the newest lighting techniques are presented for the viewer's perusal. Wherever and whenever possible, we have included schematic floor plans of the shops, as well as **comprehensive lists of the store designers, architects, consultants and suppliers.**

Selection of the photographs and editorial commentary were made by Martin M. Pegler, a recognized authority in design and visual presentation.

STORES OF THE YEAR/BOOK 4 is a large format **9"x12" hard-bound picture book with 192 pages and over 250 color photos.** Previous volumes in this collection have become a standard reference for the retail industry, therefore, **no retailer, developer, architect or designer can afford to be without this book.**

The color reproduction will enable you to grasp a feeling of "being there"—even when you're not!

$44.95
ISBN 0-934590-22-2

Here are the stores featured:

BARNEY'S, New York, NY
MISS JACKSON, Tulsa, OK
THE LIMITED, New York, NY
HUMPS, Bal Harbour, FL
BLOOMINGDALE'S, New York, NY

HENRI BENDEL, New York, NY
WOODWARD & LOTHROP, Washington, DC
NICKELS, Owing Mills, MD
EXECUTIVE LEVEL, CARSONS, Chicago, IL
ROCOCO, Pikesville, MD

ITOKIN PLAZA, King of Prussia, PA
GANTOS, Milwaukee, WI
LUNA, Bal Harbour, FL
ORMOND, Dothan, AL
ROBERT PHILLIPS, Beverly Hills, CA

MANO A MANO, New York, NY
EXECUTIVE LEVEL, CARSONS, Chicago, IL
BONWIT TELLER, New York, NY
BEAU BRUMMEL, New York, NY
TOMMY HILFIGER, New York, NY

POLITIX, Los Angeles, CA
TOP MAN, London & Watford, England
ESPRIT, Los Angeles, CA
EXPRESS, New York, NY
FIZZAZZ, New York, NY

METROPOLIS ON 2, CARSONS, Chicago, IL
WILKES SPORT, San Fran./Newport Bch., CA
JESS, Los Angeles, CA
STEFANEL, Los Angeles, CA
GOLDI, Schaumberg, IL

LEVENTHAL SHOES, Woodbury, NY
9 WEST, Ann Arbor, MI

TROPAZ, Willowbrook, NJ
BORSHEIMS, Omaha, NE
ETAGE, Tampa, FL

ACCESSORY PLACE, Livingston, NJ
IPCO SUPER OPTICAL, Lakewood, CO
PRECISION LENSCRAFTERS, Pittsburgh, PA
KOALA BLUE, Costa Mesa, CA
WEATHER STORE, New York, NY

GEAR, New York, NY
LEVEL 6, CARSONS, Chicago, IL
DANIEL HECHTER, New York, NY
COMPANY STORE, Minneapolis, MN
NEXT, London, England

THINK BIG, New York, NY
TRAVELING LIGHT, Los Angeles, CA
NORTH FACE, Costa Mesa, CA
PACIFIC MOTION, Colorado Springs, CO
HEAD, Denver, CO

KRON CHOCOLATIER, Great Neck, NY
CRABTREE & EVELYN, Escondido, CA
RECORD WORLD, Garden City, NY
BLOOMIE'S EXPRESS, JFK Airport, NY
LA SAMARITAINE, Paris, France

PARISIAN, Hoover, AL
BROADWAY, Costa Mesa, CA
HECHT'S, Washington, DC
SAKS, Palm Springs, CA
HESS, Poughkeepsie, NY

NORDSTROM, Costa Mesa, CA
ISETAN, Tokyo, Japan
HOUSE OF FRASIER, London, England
LEWIS, Leeds, England

RETAIL REPORTING 101 Fifth Avenue, New York, N.Y. 10003

Index of Stores/Shopping Centers

Index of Advertisers